# DISPLACED GENERATION

# DISPLACED GENERATION

## STORIES OF THE YOUNG, HOMELESS, AND THEIR PATHS TO HOUSING

JENNIFER PITSCH

NEW DEGREE PRESS

DISPLACED GENERATION

*Stories of the Young, Homeless, and their Paths to Housing*

ISBN    978-1-64137-334-0  *Paperback*

978-1-64137-648-8  *Ebook*

# CONTENTS

# ACKNOWLEDGEMENTS

―――

First and foremost, I would like to thank my mom, Luan Hall Pitsch, for being my biggest supporter and inspiration throughout this process. Not only are you the reason for why I started writing, but the reason I never gave up.

Thank you to my brothers, Ryan and Ben, and my Dad for your constant love and encouragement. Thank you to my best friends for cheering me on and giving me your undying support for this book through my joys and frustrations of the writing process. There are so many of you that I am lucky to have your support. Especially Alyssa, for always being my go-to for encouragement and coming along with me on occasions to hand out food to the homeless downtown, and Molly for your enthusiasm and always being there for a late-night writing sessions filled with too much coffee.

A *HUGE* thankyou to all my interviewees. You have shared your time with me, your passions, and your personal stories. I hope this book shares with others a slice of the change for good you all are adding to the world.

Thank you to all my early supporters who purchased a copy of the e-book, print book, multiple copies, or made donations: This book would not have been possible without your support in the campaign process. And thank you to everyone who spread the word about *Displaced Generation* and helped me publish a book I am proud of.

Last but not least, I would also like to acknowledge New Degree Press, especially Eric Koester, Brian Bies, my cover designer, Aleksandra Dabic, and my editors Jamie, Bailee Tracy, Gina Champagne, and Davida Smith-Keita. You made my childhood dream of writing a book come to life.

Here are the individuals who have been part of my journey:

| | |
|---|---|
| Molly Thornbrugh | John Aarons* |
| Anonymous Storytellers* | Ryan Pitsch |
| Kathy McLaughlin | Dawn Anderson |
| Lauren Brickett | Andrew Lunetta* |
| Eric Foster | Sarah Biggswudel |
| Mary Holling | Ahmar Haider* |
| Jacqueline Albers | Ryley Thomas |

Nick Courtney
Dr. Sam Tsemberis*
Pastor Tom Barber*
Melissa Bishop
Sarah Rosenkrantz*
Andy Ngo
Mikki Minton
Ben Mahoney
Jacob Parker
Beverly Rilett
Sally Guenzel
Sue Pitsch
Jana Nytch

Gail Messer
Anna Hanselman
Karen Wills
Sydney Starley
Cindy Goodin*
Kari Birnley
Jodi Pitsch
Robert Pitsch
Sean Whitten*
Kesley Coziahr
Sharene Rene
Luan Pitsch

* Interviewees

# INTRODUCTION

---

*"We have come dangerously close to accepting the homeless situation as a problem that we just can't solve."*

–LINDA LINGLE

I pushed through the tinted glass door to exit a shop in downtown Lincoln, Nebraska and was immediately drawn to the whirl of a crowd. A semi-circle of about twenty onlookers had formed down the street, a diverse crowd of males and females ranging from early twenties to late thirties. They stood silent and erect, their gaze transfixed through the recording camera lens of mobile devices held in uplifted arms.

Their silence contrasted with the sound of the commotion coming from the center of the group. I shouldered my way through until my eyes landed on a hunched over scrawny figure sitting on the ground next to the street. His straggly brown hair hung limp around his face, the messy locks shading his eyes. An oversized winter coat dwarfed him in the October breeze. Next to him, a cardboard sign lay discarded, the words, 'Homeless, anything helps,' scrawled out in shaky black ink. A trickle of scarlet blood ran down from his rapidly swelling bruised lower lip.

He leaned against a steel trash can nailed to the ground.

A male figure towered over the homeless young man. He was dressed for a night out in clean-cut jeans, a plaid shirt and a gleaming silver watch on his wrist. His face was scrunched, red cheeks puffed out as he spat out slurred profanities at the downcast face below him. He took a staggering step forward, so his waist was inches away from the face of the petrified man on the ground.

He grabbed the man by his shoulders and flung him into the steel trashcan. A thud resounded through the air as the homeless man's skull contacted steel.

Again.

Thud.

Then over and over again as the man played god over this other individual's life.

"Stop!" I screamed, rushing forward. "Why are you all just standing here? Do something!"

\*\*

The year 2016 to 2017 marks the first year in over a decade that homelessness is on the rise again.

The largest growing sub-demographic within this group was unaccompanied children and young adults at a 14.3 percent increase. [1] In fact, a survey conducted by Chapin Hall showed that one in 10 young adults ages 18–25, and one in 30 youths ages 13–17, experienced a form of homelessness over a 12-month period.[2] Millennials and younger generations face the interlocking problems of staggering debt associated with education, bleak opportunities in a tough job market, and the impact of technology and social media on both the job market and personal lives. They also, unlike previous generations, are the first that cannot remember a time that

---

1    "The State of Homelessness in America." National Alliance to End Homelessness. Accessed August 23, 2019.

2    Morton, Matthew, et al. "One in 10 Young Adults Experience Homelessness During One Year." *Chapin Hall*, Chapin Hall.

homelessness was not a part of society in the way that it is today.

To address this growing homelessness, it is important to come to terms with the reality of the situation and just how prominent it is in the nation. According to the point-in-time survey conducted by the Housing and Urban Development (HUD) department in January 2016, and reported by the National Coalition for the Homeless:[3]

- HUD found 549,928 individuals to be homeless on a single night in January 2016. Most homeless persons (65%) are individuals, while 35% of homeless persons are in family households.
- The number of families experiencing homelessness has increased significantly from past years. For example, in 2013 only 15% of homeless persons were in family households.
- **31% of all homeless people were youths under the age of 24.**
- Close to 40,000 veterans were homeless on a single night in January 2016. 66% were residing in shelters or transitional housing programs, while 33% were without shelter.

---

3    "Homelessness in America." National Coalition for the Homeless. National Coalition for the Homeless , n.d.

- The number of those in homeless shelters or transitional housing was split almost equally between people in families (47%) and individuals (53%).
- Five states, California (22%), New York (16%), Florida (6%), Texas (4%), and Washington (4%), accounted for more than half of the homeless population in the United States in 2016.
- The federal minimum wage is stagnant at $7.25 an hour. The hourly wage needed for renters hoping to afford a two-bedroom rental home is $13.96 higher than this minimum wage. In no U.S. city can a full-time minimum wage worker afford to rent a single or two bedroom home. That is because wages have stayed stagnant while housing costs have skyrocketed.
- About 1.5 million people will experience homelessness every year.

And regrettably, while homelessness is on the rise, a corresponding lack of empathy for the homeless has come with it. In fact, "*Bum Fights*" has become a popular user-generated show on YouTube. The *Bum Fights* film series featured the homeless engaging in stunts such as fighting each other, drinking urine, being set on fire, or terrorized by a man called the 'Bum Hunter.' After the initial series took off, many copycats films followed, with people terrorizing homeless in their own community. In some cases, this even led to the homeless individual's death.

At a time when more needs to be done to curb the challenges with homelessness, people are pulling away from the problem.

**

The man swung again at the now huddled figure, his lip now split wide open.

My scream fell on deaf ears.

Nobody so much as looked at me as I took a hesitant step forward, suddenly all too aware of how my 5'6" frame and lack of muscles from twenty-one years of avoiding physical activity at all costs, stacked up against this 6'3" enraged drunk.

A weight on my left arm pulled me back. I whipped my head around to the widened eyes of my friend.

"We need to turn the other way and get out of this situation," she pleaded as she tugged me further out of the danger of the inner circle.

In that moment, my feelings of anger and injustice gave way to another one: powerlessness. I played out the scenarios of me walking up to that one-sided fight and I knew that logically each one of them ended with me either pushed to the side or physically assaulted.

"We can't just leave." The defeat in my voice was clear even to me. As I glanced around, nobody had moved from their stationary positions, even the individuals who could have physically intimidated this abuser. Seconds that felt like an eternity ticked forward.

Groans escaped the battered homeless young man.

Around the corner, I spotted a cop.

Relief washed over me as my friend and I yelled at him to help.

He strolled over and finally grabbed the abuser, circling his arms around him.

He forced the man to put both arms behind his back.

"I was just asking for a cigarette," he said as the cop led him away. People dispersed. The assaulted young man was left huddled next to the trash clutching his sign, bleeding, powerless, and once again unseen.

**

I wanted to write this book after seeing young homelessness in my own community, but even more so after I witnessed that scene of general apathy by my own peers. The violence

I witnessed in my own community could have been stopped. But every bystander only stood transfixed, their phones out and recording for the next big Snapchat story, tweet, or Facebook post.

Homelessness is not going away and in fact is increasing.

When we look back a few decades ago to the early 1970s, scholars, such as Anthony Jackson, were quoted saying, "No Western democracy could possibly get away with letting its citizens fall through the cracks into homelessness." Before the 1970s, homelessness rose and fell with the economic state of the country, but after, there was a drastic and permanent rise in homelessness.

This new homelessness is chronic and hits minorities, women, and blue-collar workers the hardest.

And yet our empathy for the homeless may be at an all-time low.

The incident I witnessed is all too reminiscent of the kind of problems that happen on a grander scale and stream on news outlets and social media. When people document incidents in a well-intentioned way, such as to spread news and raise awareness, they are often stalled along the path to fixing the problem. People spread the news, discuss it with their peers, and then go about their day. That's it; the extent we extend our comfort zone in order to solve the problem has turned into nothing more than a general awareness. The surer path to making progress involves both an active awareness and a fundamental understanding of the complex causes of the issue at hand, then research and brainstorming of possible solutions that can be undertaken, and finally implementation of these effective and evidence-based solutions that seem to be the best choice.

Those possible solutions are featured in this book, as well as chapters that break down misconceptions regarding the young homeless. In this book, you'll learn about why homeless youth are afraid of homeless shelters, and what alternatives are out there, as well as different types of methodologies to address youth homelessness. One of these was formulated by the Rapid Results Institute. The Rapid Results Institute works to eradicate youth homelessness in just 100 days. The story of how they do that is examined in these pages. Then there are also heartwarming stories such as Kate's. Kate became an unintentional community activist when she opened her house as a safe home to over thirty boys in just under four years.

**

Unlike that moment when I felt helpless watching a homeless young man beaten and bloodied, I've realized I can help. This book aims to offer a new look—told through fresh perspectives gathered from dozens of experts and innovators undertaking this growing problem.

I don't have the answer, but I do believe without active and caring conversations happening we may never get closer to those answers.

This book lays out what I believe is the fundamental causes of youth and young adult homelessness, many of which are not what you may expect. It also presents what innovative solutions researchers, community leaders, legislators, and non-profits across the US and beyond are trying out. It also explains common overlooked problems that are specific to youth and young adult homelessness, such as why adult shelters may not be the best answer, and the issues with juggling both education and housing insecurity.

Youth homelessness does not have to be our future.

Young adult and youth homelessness can be reversed, if people are given the right tools and knowledge to know how to deal with it. As this book outlines, this problem is so wide-ranging that there is no one clear cut, fix-all Band-Aid, but some methods are clearly more effective than others.

While Linda Lingle said, "We have come dangerously close to accepting the homeless situation as a problem that we just can't solve," her statement offers a glimmer of hope.

Join me to find that hope.

# THE FACE OF HOMELESSNESS

———

## A BRIEF HISTORY OF U.S. HOMELESSNESS

Their loose-fit tattered blue jeans are pulled up to their waist. They peer up from under the hood of their oversized winter coat and offer a toothy smile that highlights the creases and smears of dirt on their weathered faces. Black plastic trash bags line the wall behind them, stuffed to the brim with clothes, a blanket, food, and whatever other necessities they can fit. If they are lucky, they have found an abandoned shopping cart that these belongings can be stuffed into when they are forced to make a hasty exit by public authority or nearby danger. This person gestures with one hand for you to look at the cardboard where the words, 'Homeless Please Help,' are scrawled out in black marker.

What did you imagine this person to look like? If you thought an elder, grizzly male you are not alone. Many also imagine empty alcohol bottles haplessly cast to the side, the smell of weed and cigarettes hovering in the air. However, the face of homelessness has changed rapidly, and this description is more likely to describe a diverse range of people of differing gender, races, and ages. Minorities and those in the LGBTQA group make up an overrepresented portion of the demographic.

Pastor Tom Barber is all too familiar with the stereotypes that the homeless face. As CEO of the People's City Mission, a Lincoln, Nebraska based homeless shelter, he has been at the forefront of helping a diverse set of individuals transition through their shelter's doors: "I definitely think there is a stigma with being in a homeless shelter, of being elder, transient men. When in reality anybody can be homeless."

Many people are stuck imagining the way homelessness was depicted from past generations. This involved the hobos traveling by railroad journeying to find work, or scrounging for money on the streets. Often, what's left out of the picture is the young who have always dealt with homelessness, even if it was not at the same levels of today.

## POST-CIVIL WAR ERA

Young adults have always had a relationship with homelessness. In fact, homelessness was first coined as a term in the 1870s to describe the group of young, able-bodied, mostly white men who cropped up in response to the railroad system, riding it in search of jobs. After a brief lull in homelessness right after the Civil War, homelessness became a national issue due to the combined forces of industrialization, urbanization, mobility, and the construction of the railroad system.[4]

The new railroad system coupled with the end of the Civil War left many jobless and in search of a wage. War veterans came back from the war unable to find employment while others lost their property after it had been taken in war or lost to natural catastrophes. The culmination of these factors led to widespread economic dislocation.

The view of these citizens was not favorable. In urban locations such as New York, the homeless rose in response to the economic recession. The media widely covered these individuals as 'tramps' and 'vagrants' who were a threat to their civilization.

---

4    National Academies of Sciences. "The History of Homelessness in the United States." Permanent Supportive Housing: Evaluating the Evidence for Improving Health Outcomes Among People Experiencing Chronic Homelessness. July 11, 2018. Accessed July 01, 2019.

"At the present time there is supposed to be at least 3,000 vagrants in this City, while there is a large number who travel from place to place, either begging as they go along, or doing odd jobs for their meals," quoted a *New York Times* article from December of 1873, "These tramps are always pretending to look for work, but it is very rare that they will accept it if offered, unless to get a chance to steal something."[5]

Institutionalized racism also contributed to homelessness targeting specific segments of the population. Emerging racism gave minorities unequal access in attaining jobs.

## THE GREAT DEPRESSION

Later, 'boxcar girls and boys' rose in response to the Great Depression between the years 1929–1941. Teenagers were forced to forsake their way of life, possessions, and home to ride the rails. Forced from their homes onto the tracks in search of a job, food, and some semblance of lodging, these young hobos accounted for 250,000 of the four million Americans struggling to survive.

Many accounts that detailed their journeys from that period added a quality of romanticism. The image of the locomotive accelerating across the tracks of the wild west of the

---

5   "28 Dec 1873, Page 5 – The New York Times at Newspapers.com." Newspapers.com. Accessed July 01, 2019.

American countryside seemed picturesque. Details like the rush of the locomotive, young teenager's adrenaline pumping from train jumping, the screech from steam escaping the locomotive blast pipe, made it out to be an adventure that brings a sense of nostalgia similar to the wild American West.

Yet, another side to the story covers the hunger, desperation, and poverty that pushed these young individuals to take up root on the boxcars initially, along with the daily dangers they faced. Daniel Elliot was a twelve-year-old riding with his dad to find work. In a letter he explained he stopped riding after he lost a dear friend who fell off the freight car and was found the next morning.[6] Others, in their wild attempt to secure a spot on the boxcars, lost legs that had to be amputated.

Samm Coombs was only fourteen when he rode the rail. The transition of moving from car to car was extremely dangerous and unlike anything these teenagers had experienced before.

"At no time and at no place, during war or peace, feast or famine, have I experienced anything that scared me as totally and completely as looking down between those first two cars,

---

6    "The Boxcar Boys and Girls." Hobo Life in the Great Depression. 2016.

at those big steel wheels rolling over that shiny steel track and seeing my almost-15-year-old self lying there like a platter of sliced turkey," Coombs said.[7]

These children had to survive on meager sustenance, sometimes going without food for days or eating mold-riddled rations. Archie Lawson, a twenty-one-year-old California resident when he left for the road, recalled the experience of starvation during this time and how humbling it was:

"I went into a store and asked for "something to eat." But it was not that simple! It was an emotional, shameful thing that is almost impossible for me to explain. I was practically crying, my face was red, I felt defeated."[8]

## POST-WWII

Besides the hobos and wanderers that came along with the aftermath of war and recession, homelessness was still not recognized as the sort of street-living that came later. Part of the reason was that after the Great Depression, homelessness was not the issue it is in modern times. The post-war 1950s through 1970s experienced a boom in the economy that shrunk the gap between the poor and the rich. Even into the

7   Ibid
8   Ibid

1970s, people believed that Western society would not let its citizens fall through the cracks based on poverty.

As mentioned in the introduction, scholar Anthony Jackson in 1976 credibly wrote that, "The housing industry trades on the knowledge that no Western country can politically afford to permit its citizens to sleep in the streets." [9]

This post WWII era illustrated how homelessness rose and fell in accordance with the state of the economy. The better the economy was doing, the less unemployment there typically was, and in return the less homelessness existed. When the economy was in a downturn and a state of high unemployment, the homeless levels would rise. After this period though, and into the 1970s, the level of displaced people changed. It increased and was less cyclical and more likely to be chronic. The reasoning for this was a conglomerate of factors including government policy, urbanization, and the state of the housing market.

---

9    Jackson A. A Place Called Home: A History of Low–Cost Housing in Manhattan. Cambridge, MA: MIT Press; 1976.

## THE 1980S TO 2000S

Homelessness in the 1980s was worsened by several factors that impacted youths and young adults: more demand than supply for affordable housing options, the gentrification of housing, and budget cuts to social programs and the U.S. Department of Housing & Urban Development.[10]

### AFFORDABLE HOUSING OPTIONS

The housing market was rapidly changing in the 1970s-80s decades. Although the nation's population continued to increase, 45 million houses were taken off the housing market in this decade; most of these homes belonged to low-income families and individuals.[11] The public housing program dis-

---

10   Jones, Marian Moser. "Creating a Science of Homelessness During the Reagan Era." *The Milbank Quarterly* 93, no. 1 (March 2015): 139–78. https://doi.org/10.1111/1468–0009.12108.

11   Blasi, Gary, Dan Flaming, Michael Dear, Paul Koegel, Paul Tepper, Daniel Warshawsky, and Jennifer Wolch. "What Led to the Rise of Homelessness." KCET. April 06, 2017. Accessed July 01,

appeared with programs such as Section 8 housing vouchers meant to replace them, but this program only had a slight effect on the affordable housing available.

### GENTRIFICATION OF HOUSING

Gentrification describes the process of wealthier residents moving into neighborhoods of less wealthy occupants and the effects that come along with this. Gentrification has been touted for its remaking of previously 'bad' neighborhoods into cleaner, safer, more well-educated zones. In New York City, for example, think of the remaking of Brooklyn from dangerous and poverty-stricken to the hipster, millennial culture it boasts today.

Yet, not all effects of gentrification are good. By moving in richer residents as a fix to the neighborhoods, it does not relieve the poverty for the people already there. Rather, for many, it exacerbates their situation as they fight to maintain affordable housing over rising rent rates. Where gentrification has hit the hardest was in urban areas.

A study conducted in 1982 found that in the US, 1 percent of Americans, 5 percent of families, and 8.5 percent of urban families were displaced during the years 1970–1977 through

2019. https://www.kcet.org/shows/socal-connected/the-rise-of-homelessness-in-the-1980s.

eviction, sale or reoccupation, or public action.[12] A different study in 1983 showed nearly a quarter of residents in five cities-Boston, Cincinnati, Denver, Richmond, and Seattle— were displaced due to gentrification of their neighborhoods.[13]

## BUDGET CUTS

Then in 1982 through 1985, there was a cutback of $57 billion from federal programs whose objective related to reducing poverty. As a result most working families enrolled on federal Aid to Families with Dependent Children program were dropped.[14]

"One of the first things Reagan did was to stop the Department of Housing and Urban Development, from building affordable housing, the way that they had been doing for many, many years before that. So that program just went away. And it's never been never been re-instituted. This country used to build around 350,000 units of affordable housing every year. During the early Reagan years, that dropped to about 50,000, where it has remained all this time," said Dr. Sam Tsemberis, founder of Pathways to Housing.

---

12  Newman, Sandra J., and Michael S. Owen. "Residential Displacement: Extent, Nature, and Effects." *Journal of Social Issues* 38, no. 3 (1982): 135–48. doi:10.1111/j.1540–4560.1982.tb01775.x.
13  Vertz, Laura L. *Publius* 15, no. 1 (1985): 183–85. http://www.jstor.org/stable/3329956.
14  Newman and Owen. "Residential Displacement,"

These policies led to a decrease in affordable housing. People who are not making a lot of money have a much harder time finding affordable units. Added to this, housing, since the 1980s, has gone into a huge boom. Housing has become a commodity with all kinds of people investing and building housing on the market with hedge funds, pension funds, and stock commodities. Subsequently, rents have risen higher and higher. At the same time people's wages have not kept up at that same level of escalation, except for the very wealthy.

## A DIVERSE POPULATION

This new face of homelessness was different in that it incorporated more women, African Americans, and young people than before. No longer was it mainly an assemblage of single, alcoholic, aged, white males.

The 1980s marked not only an uprising in homelessness, but homelessness becoming a social issue in the eye of the public. There was issue taken, however, in determining if the underlying cause was due more to mental illness or if it was economic events and policies that were the cause, such as a recession and cutbacks in social programs. Without knowing the cause, focusing on what policies to push for was impossible.

Marian Moser Jones in her research has noted that by looking at the subgroup demographics of homelessness the problem was not a mental illness problem. Yet, federal and private enterprises lacked substantial research into why so many people were homeless without a substance abuse problem or mental illness.

Intertwined with the history of youth homelessness is how that dilemma has been framed to the public. Before the word 'homelessness' caught on to the public the homeless were little more than two-dimensional archetypes. The crazy bag lady with the grocery cart, the stumbling drunk man with a mid-life crisis, the crouched-over druggie shooting up in an alleyway. When humans are framed in this snapshot, it is easier for society to say, 'That is an individual problem; their homelessness is caused by their own addiction, drug abuse, mental illness, and that is a *them* problem not an *us* problem.'

In reality, as will be shown, this is not what is going on in the youth subgroup. Often the addiction and mental health issues they face are the outcome rather than the cause of homelessness.

Instead there needs to be a reframing of youth and young adult homelessness from "a problem of persons" to "a problem of place, resources, political economy, power, and market failure," as the late professor Michael Katz wrote.[15]

What became a catalyst for the perspective change of the homeless was a 1981 *New York Times* article by Ellen Baxter and Kim Hopper titled, "Help Is Urged for 36,000 Homeless in City's Streets." At this point the media did not refer to this group by a consistently neutral title. Generally, the terms bum, vagrant, drifter, tramp were all negatively perceived words that implied there was an individual quality about these people that put them where they were, for example, laziness.

In sociologist Marian Moser Jones's interviews with Hopper and Baxter the two reflected on how their word choice was intentional: They looked to reframe the center issue as one fixated on the lack of affordable housing more than one of mental health, individual decision, or an individual's failures socially.[16]

---

15  Katz, Michael B. *The Undeserving Poor: From the War on Poverty to the War on Welfare.* New York: Pantheon Book, 1989.

16  Jones, Marian Moser. "Creating a Science of Homelessness During the Reagan Era." *The Milbank Quarterly* 93, no. 1 (March 2015): 139–78. https://doi.org/10.1111/1468–0009.12108.

Their strategic advocacy succeeded in the adoption of word usage by the media outlets, journalists, politicians, and researchers. No longer was this diverse group initially defined by negative qualities they do not all carry or addiction problems alone rather than the economic issues that put them on the streets.

## THE GREAT RECESSION TO TODAY

The Great Recession in 2008, like any extreme low in the business cycle, caused unemployment to increase and homelessness too as a result. During the initial time-period, the collapse of the housing bubble caused a ripple effect. July through November of 2008, the number of families in the New York homeless shelters increased by 40 percent compared to the same time-period the previous year.[17] A national survey reported one in five responding school districts had more homeless children in the fall of 2008 than over the course of the entire 2007–2008 school year.[18]

---

17   Sand, Barbara. "Number of Homeless Families Climbing Due To Recession." Center on Budget and Policy Priorities. October 11, 2017. Accessed July 01, 2019. https://www.cbpp.org/research/number-of-homeless-families-climbing-due-to-recession.

18   Barbara Duffield and Phillip Lovell, "The Economic Crisis Hits Home: The Unfolding Increase in Child and Youth Homelessness," National Association for the Education of Homeless Children and Youth and First Focus, December 2008.

Yet what could have turned into increasing heights in homelessness following 2008 was an almost complete stagnation in the numbers of homeless people between 2008 to 2012. To explain this, it is important to look at the economic effects of a housing market collapse and how the federal government intervened.

Homelessness is not directly related to poverty. In some of the poorest areas of the nation, such as Alabama and Mississippi, the homelessness level is low because the cost of housing remains cheaper than popular places where people choose to live such as metropolitan cities. Because the collapse of the housing market drove prices downward, one of the effects was basic shelter was affordable to a higher number of individuals, especially in these rural areas.[19]

Another factor that ended up driving down homelessness was the federal government policies. Back in 2010 the Obama administration made a pledge to end homelessness in a decade, by the year 2020. HUD estimated that there were 637,077 homeless in the U.S. in their point-in-time count for 2010. The plan, called, "Opening Doors," a "Federal Strategic Plan to Prevent and End Homelessness," was the first

19  Horowitz, Evan. "Poverty Drives Homeless Rates? Not so Fast – The Boston Globe." BostonGlobe.com. August 24, 2016. Accessed July 01, 2019. https://www.bostonglobe.com/2016/08/24/poverty-drives-homeless-rates-fast/1fvvSKgNUg4l5TfqbdEGrM/story.html.

federal guideline with a detailed timeline and goals on how to approach this problem.[20] It seemed to be working in the economy—for a time.

The plan adopted policy concepts such as Housing First and Rapid Re-housing, which started at the local level and saw widespread success.

Within six years the country saw double digit percentage drops in homelessness among families, individuals experiencing homelessness, and veterans. While in some states, such as New York, the percentage of homelessness rose, the nation saw a 14 percent decrease in homelessness by 2016. The homeless point-in-time count by the HUD in 2016 had dropped down to 549,928.[21]

But homelessness is once again on the rise. For the first time in seven years, homelessness has increased nationally by 0.7 percent in the 2016 to 2017 period. The largest increases

20  Newspapers, Tony Pugh – McClatchy. "Obama Vows to End Homelessness in 10 Years." McClatchy DC. June 22, 2010. Accessed July 09, 2019. https://www.mcclatchydc.com/news/nation-world/national/economy/article24585973.html.
21  Capps, Kriston. "Nationwide, Homelessness Plunged Under Obama." CityLab. November 18, 2016. Accessed July 09, 2019. https://www.citylab.com/equity/2016/11/homelessness-obama-trump/508223/.

were among the demographic of unaccompanied children and young adults.[22]

In individual cities and populations, there has also been an increasing trend towards homeless youth living in completely unsheltered locations versus having at least a shelter, car, abandoned building or other cover to stay. In San Diego, there was a 39 percent jump in 2017 of homeless youth. In Atlanta, the number of homeless youth tripled over previous years, most shockingly, Seattle's King County jumped by over 700 percent between 2012 and 2015. Unaccompanied youth in public schools also increased by a fifth between 2012–2015.[23]

During this time there have been proposed budget cuts to HUD from the president:

The Trump administration proposed to slash the HUD budget by 13.2 percent or about $6.2 billion in FY 2018.[24] Congress

---

22  "The State of Homelessness in America." National Alliance to End Homelessness. Accessed July 09, 2019. https://endhomelessness.org/homelessness-in-america/homelessness-statistics/state-of-homelessness-report-legacy/.

23  Wiltz, Teresa. "A Hidden Population: Youth Homelessness Is on the Rise." The Pew Charitable Trusts. July 7, 2017. Accessed July 09, 2019. https://www.pewtrusts.org/en/research-and-analysis/blogs/stateline/2017/07/07/a-hidden-population-youth-homelessness-is-on-the-rise.

24  Ramírez, Kelsey. "Proposed 2020 HUD Budget Sees Meager Increase from Last Year's Proposal." HousingWire.com. March 11, 2019. Accessed July 09, 2019. https://www.housingwire.com/

has rejected the proposals, electing to increase the budget each year. The 2018 funding was increased by 4.7 billion, or about 10 percent above the 2017 year. Yet, adjusted for inflation, these increases have not put the budget back at the level it was during the 2010 era.[25]

Most recently, HUD, in their 2018 Annual Homeless Assessment Report to Congress, reported its second increase in the homeless point-in-time count from 550,996 to 552,830 in 2017 to 2018.[26]

"Most people who are under 30 have no idea that the country was a very different country before the 1980s. Homelessness was not part of the landscape as it is today. Not only do we have homeless people, but we've developed an entire industry of services to take care of the homeless," said Dr. Tsemberis. "That's all relatively recent."

articles/48396-proposed-2020-hud-budget-sees-meager-increase-from-last-years-proposal.

25  Bell, Alison, and Douglas Rice. "Congress Prioritizes Housing Programs in 2018 Funding Bill, Rejects Trump Administration Proposals." Center on Budget and Policy Priorities. July 20, 2018. Accessed July 09, 2019. https://www.cbpp.org/research/housing/congress-prioritizes-housing-programs-in-2018-funding-bill-rejects-trump.

26  Henry, Meghan, Anna Mahathey, Tyler Morrill, Anna Robinson, Azim Shivji, Rian Watt, and Abt Associates. *The 2018 Annual Homeless Assessment Report (AHAR) to Congress.* Report. The U.S. Department of Housing and Urban Development. 2018.

# THE ROOT OF
# THE PROBLEM

———

*Names have been changed to preserve anonymity

Kate* was introduced to the risks that homeless youth face by an unconventional route. Her three high-school aged sons had friends in troubled situations and wanted to help. Kate's home soon developed an open-door policy and even more importantly, a second family. Kate, or Mama Kate as the boys referred to her, had over thirty-two boys stay at her home throughout the years whenever they needed a place to get away or someone who cared to listen.

Michael* was one of the youth who stayed with Kate's family. He, like many other peers his age, was living with circumstances out of his control. He had a dad who had been in prison since before he was born. His mom was an alcoholic and his two little sisters were addicted to meth at the ages of 15 and 16. His mom went from one relationship to the next, following a pattern of dating men who were alcoholic and abusive. Michael's grandparents lived in a town that was too far for him to commute to every day to get to school. And so, Michael began a strategy of avoidance. Whenever his mom was in a relationship, he would stay with Kate's family for a couple weeks at a time.

The final straw came when Michael's mom said she wanted him to meet her most recent boyfriend. Michael went home from Kate's place and walked in on an unforgettable scene. The boyfriend had his mom off the floor with his hands around her throat. Her face was turning blue.

"So, as any self-respecting 16-year-old boy would do, desperate to protect his mom, he jumped on that guy and started to beat the crap out of him. I mean, literally beat the stuffing out of that guy. His mom fell on the floor. As soon as she regained consciousness, she screamed at her son and said, 'Don't you dare beat up my boyfriend,'" said Kate.

In response, Michael yelled, 'Mom the guy was choking you out.' His mom didn't care, but only pounded on Michael's back to break up the fight. 'Fine,' he said, 'Forget it. I'm done.'

He went to his room, grabbed his bedspread, and threw his belongings into it. But the boyfriend, whom he had come over to meet, had grabbed a gun in the meantime and came after Michael, who raced out the door and across the yard, the gun-toting boyfriend in pursuit.

"Michael came to my house and said, Mom [Kate], I'm done. I'm not staying for two weeks at a time. Now I'm really done. I can't live with my mom anymore," said Kate.

"Michael was really, really new to me. And I said, I know you don't like to be hugged, but, you're exempt this time. He looked me in the face and said, 'It's okay, I don't get hugs much where I come from, you can hug me anytime you want to.' That just dropped me to my knees. Even now, when he is twenty-five, every time I see him, I get at least a thirty-two second hug and he just stands there in my hug."

There are many such youth around the nation who live in family situations similar to Michael's. In fact, there are around 1.3 million youth runaways that have chosen the streets. They live huddled against walls and concrete curbs, in abandoned homes, or with friends or strangers.[27] Most are not lucky enough to know a family like Kate's who greet

---

27  "Youth Homelessness Overview." National Conference of State Legislatures. June 18, 2019. http://www.ncsl.org/research/human-services/homeless-and-runaway-youth.aspx.

them with open arms. These kids have the untenable choice between living in an abusive family situation or running away to live on the streets.

## CAUSES OF YOUTH HOMELESSNESS

To solve the problem of youth homelessness you must first determine what is causing it. Each individual case is different, but common themes run through most of them. These include issues such as conflicts within the family, poverty, and housing insecurity, juvenile and justice system involvement, and residential instability.

A report done by the Administration on Children, Youth and Families, Family and Youth Services Bureau showed that when asked why youths first became homeless, results showed that 51 percent said they had been asked to leave home or kicked out; 25 percent said they could not find a job; 24 percent said it was because they had been physically abused or beaten; 23 percent said it was due to a caregiver's drug or alcohol use, 13 percent said it was due to their own drug or alcohol use, and 7 percent said it was attributed to exiting jail or prison.[28]

---

28  Administration on Children, Youth and Families, Family and Youth Services Bureau: Street Outreach Program Data Collection Project Final Report (April 2016).

## UNSTABLE FAMILY SITUATIONS

The number one reason youths, specifically ages 12 to 18, end up homeless is disruptive family situations.[29] These children want to escape situations that involve physical or sexual abuse and exploitation, family that have substance abuse problems, or parental neglect. In other cases, youth are asked or forced to leave by parents who do not feel capable of caring for them. One study by HUD researchers showed that more than half of the youth interviewed at homeless shelters reported they left because their parents either told them to or these parents knew and did not care.[30]

Another study reported that 46 percent of runaway and homeless youth reported being physically abused, 38 percent reported being emotionally abused, and 17 percent reported being forced into unwanted sexual activity by a family or household member.'[31]

---

29  "Homeless Youth: NCH Fact Sheet #13." National Coalition for the Homeless, August 2007. https://www.nationalhomeless.org/publications/facts/youth.pdf.

30  U.S. Department of Health and Human Services(a). Youth with Runaway, Throwaway, and Homeless Experiences… Prevalence Drug Use, and Other At-Risk Behaviors, 1995. Volume I (the Final Report, including the executive summary) is available for $48.15; the Executive Summary alone is available for $3.15. Order from the National Clearinghouse on Families & Youth, P. O. Box 13505, Silver Spring, MD 20911–3505; 301–608–8098.

31  "Youth Homelessness Overview." National Conference of State Legislatures.

James is one of these young individuals. He stayed with his mom until her drug addiction and physical abuse by other family members made them part ways.

"I was living with my mom. [...] I thought we had a bond, a strong connection but we really didn't. She ended up putting crack before me, she ended letting her own brother put his hands on me, beating me up really badly. She ended up putting me out."[32]

He tried to relocate to other family members he thought would welcome him—his cousin and grandparents—but in both cases it didn't work out. The family problems at home continued and worsened until he relocated to Chicago. He was sleeping on porches, under bushes or on the streets, anywhere he could find a place to rest for the night. In James' case he got lucky and found help in the form of a supportive youth shelter, but not all young homeless individuals are so fortunate.

Other family conflicts involve an unsupportive environment over a young person's choices or actions. Between 20 and 40% of homeless youth identify as part of the LGBTQA (Lesbian,

---

32 "James Was Living with Him Mom until Drugs Forced Him out into the Chicago Streets." Interview by Mark Horvath. YouTube. September 19, 2013. https://www.youtube.com/watch?v=9mzGuBWR0-3Q&list=PL51CPD51hq2Qk3M5TV50Gac9GsyHouSa3&index=24.

Gay, Bi-sexual, Transgender, Questioning, Asexual) community. Often, these individuals' coming out stories ended with families that could not accept them, or they felt the need to leave to stay true to themselves.

Bobby Berk, now famous from Netflix's show *Queer Eye*, was one of these youth. He grew up in a household where views on gay people forced him into a traumatic situation of choosing between his identity or acceptance from his family, extended loved ones, and his tightly knit small community.

"[I was taught] that gay people were bad, they were pedophiles, they were evil," Bobby said on the show. "So, I spent every prayer meeting on every Sunday crying and begging God to not make me gay." [33]

Berk ran away from his small-town home in Mount Vernon when he was only fifteen. Most surprisingly, he lamented that he did not come out to his family at the time that he ran away. It wasn't until his interview on Jonathan Van Ness's podcast, (his *Queer Eye* co-star) that Bobby Berk went into depth with his origin story and why he ran away.

"I was fifteen. You know I lived in a very religious family. I lived in a very small religious town. And a lot of people were

---

33   "Camp Rules." Transcript. In *Queer Eye*. Netflix. February 7, 2018.

like, 'Oh you left because you were gay, your parents kicked you out.' My parents did not kick me out, but I knew that I could not come out and stay home, and I could not come out and stay in the town I lived in." [34]

Berk went on to share how another boy at his religious high school of approximately three hundred students came out. He was terrorized afterward. At one point a group of students ran him off the road and almost killed him. Bobby felt that after these events, coming out was not an option in his hometown.

After running away, Berk lived on the streets, crashed at friends' places in Springfield, and slept in his car, struggling to survive on the money he made as an Applebee's employee.[35]

"I used to live in my car in Branson, Missouri [...] and the Applebee's parking lot, because I would work all day at Applebee's on Thursdays and then I would sleep in my car on Thursday night. I'd work all day Friday, sleep in my car, work all day Saturday, sleep in my car then work all day Sunday. Then

---

34  Bobby, Berk. "What's Your Origin Story? with Bobby Berk." Interview by Jonathan Van Ness. *Getting Curious with Jonathan Van Ness* (audio blog), July 24, 2018.

35  Gleeson, Jill. "A Home Full of Hope: Bobby Berk." EDGE Media Network. November 27, 2014. Accessed July 09, 2019. https://www.edgemedianetwork.com/style/home//168738.

I would drive back to Springfield to like stay with friends on their sofas."[36]

**

Similar to Berk's situation, Pastor Tom Barber, CEO of People's City Mission, has realized in his experience that solving the problem with youth homelessness has to involve more than just the youth:

"The problem with solving youth homeless is they are attached to the parent. A lot of families are dysfunctional—drugs, breaking up, social problems—youth homelessness is the end tail of this. To get to the root of the problem you have to look at the family," said Pastor Tom.

Dropping off homeless youth at the doorstep of the home where they first left leaves the initial dynamic unresolved. To stop the revolving door of running, it is necessary to create a stable family environment where the young individual feels safe. Youth who have run once have already made the choice that they would rather risk the dangers of living on the streets than the instability, danger, or unacceptance they feel at home.

---

36  Bobby, Berk. "What's Your Origin Story?"

## JUVENILE SYSTEM INVOLVEMENT

David cycled between the juvenile system and homelessness over a dozen times during his minor years. He was only thirteen when he first landed on the streets, before then he bounced between divorced parents and a family friend.

"I'd get out of Juvie and I'd already know, well, I'm going to be back to Juvie soon," said David. "But what I didn't know was how to not be homeless."[37]

David was involved in a variety of illegal activities by his high school years. He'd handled guns and smoked methamphetamine. During this time, he had a parole officer, but her options for the potential runaway and homeless was limited to recommending shelters in the region for him to stay.

There exists a complex relationship between homeless youth and the justice system. Whether they got into trouble before or during their homeless period, the two factors have an interlocking impact on each other. A study that looked at

---

37   Abramo, Allegra. "Youth Often Become Homeless Just after Leaving Juvenile Detention. Can Washington State Really Stop It?" The Seattle Times. April 25, 2019. Accessed July 09, 2019. https://www.seattletimes.com/seattle-news/homeless/youth-often-become-homeless-just-after-leaving-juvenile-detention-can-state-really-stop-it/.

homeless youth in 11 cities found that 44 percent had stayed in jail, a juvenile detention center, or prison; 77 percent had run-ins with the police, and nearly 62 percent had been arrested at some point.[38]

The precarious situations of these youth, (poverty, family issues, or abuse) may lead to theft of food, money, or other necessities when there is no money. Truancy becomes an issue when the youth exceeds the allowed number of school days missed. Unsafe living situations or living on the streets might result in a child lashing out in a fight at school and a subsequent assault charge.

These run-ins with the justice system can make a youth who is not already homeless more likely to be. For example, educational disruptions and juvenile delinquency records can make finding employment more difficult.[39] Juvenile Court involvement can also be a risk factor that points to someone already on the edge of unstable home conditions.

---

38  Administration on Children, Youth and Families, Family and Youth Services Bureau: Street Outreach Program Data Collection Project Final Report (April 2016).

39  Pilnik, Lisa, Darla Bardine, Laura Furr, Meghan Maury, Melissa Sickmund, Naomi Smoot, and Jason Szanyi. *Addressing the Intersections of Juvenile Justice Involvement and Youth Homelessness: Principles for Change.*Report. March 2017. https://www.csh.org/wp-content/uploads/2017/03/Principles_FINAL.pdf.

## ECONOMIC POVERTY

Another type of youth homelessness is caused by economic poverty that forces the family unit onto the streets. In these situations, the youth are not necessarily in conflict with their parents. Their parents are experiencing homelessness alongside them due to economic circumstances. The financial circumstances that push these families into homelessness can be lack of affordable housing, inability to maintain a steady job or one that pays a living wage, or no fallback funds or programs when a family experiences tough setbacks.

Although these youth experience homelessness with their family, sometimes they can be separated due to child welfare policies or shelter policies that do not accommodate families, children over a certain age, or single fathers.[40] Shelters that have family spaces are often limited and do not meet the demand.

In the case of an Oakland family of five, it was the overwhelming and eventually insurmountable cost of medical bills. The mother, Aisha, experienced life-threatening pneumonia and a collapsed lung after giving birth to her newborn which led to many months in the hospital. Aisha was an event planner for a medical device company. Her husband, Ezra,

---

40 "Youth Homelessness Overview." National Conference of State Legislatures. June 18, 2019. http://www.ncsl.org/research/human-services/homeless-and-runaway-youth.aspx.

was a sound technician. Ezra took time off work to take care of the new baby and eventually lost his job.

Seventeen-year-old daughter Tamia said the situation was eye-opening. "A lot of people are one incident, one accident, one job loss away from the same situation."

Tamia's family has been sleeping in their family car since the eviction from their apartment. They have no kitchen, no bathroom, and inadequate storage space. Their mornings begin with fast food, then a search for a public restroom to clean up before school. During this time, their sixteen-year-old son Jonathan's grades plummeted. Juggling school work, no home, and food and financial insecurity is something children are ill-equipped to handle physically or emotionally.[41]

## RESIDENTIAL INSTABILITY

A fourth contributor to youth homelessness stems from residential and institutional conditions. As foster care providers change, children and youth must navigate new environments. Other young individuals are placed in institutional settings. When these youth reach the age upon which they are discharged from institutions or are aged out of foster care, they

---

41 "Oakland Homeless Family." Interview. YouTube. August 10, 2017. Accessed July 9, 2019. https://www.youtube.com/watch?v=zo5kHGeWULM.

often end up homeless. They lack the income to support themselves and find that the demand for adequate shelters far exceeds the supply.

Jacob grew up in foster care. He was moved to four different places over the course of his childhood. His upbringing and life in the foster system was negative. He described his experience as akin to being in, 'kid prisons.' He lamented that he was not taught basic and necessary life skills such as financial expenses and even how to tell time.

"I was aged out of foster care; you just age out. You turn eighteen and the world just says, 'Okay you are an adult now, go and fend for yourself. [...] I was homeless ever since. No one ever told me how to write a check. I don't know the first thing about expenses, renting an apartment. [...] I couldn't tell time till I was seventeen. I mean I had a watch, but it was just for show."[42]

On his eighteenth birthday, the foster care home he was staying at kicked him out. They told him to pack up his bags and leave, the state wasn't paying for him anymore. He spent his birthday on a trek down the streets until he came to a gas station, met a bum, and was taught how to panhandle. That

---

42 "Homeless Youth Aged out of Foster Care." Interview by Mark Horvath. YouTube. September 2, 2013. Accessed July 9, 2019. https://www.youtube.com/watch?v=TbquG1HoCXQ.

man connected him to other homeless. The reality becomes homeless youth turned young adults who start their journey with this institutional birthday present. Legal adulthood for them is akin to the loss of any sort of support from the government or welfare programs.

Charles is another young adult who went through the foster care system starting at the young age of eight. He cycled through twenty-five different homes before the age of sixteen when he finally he ran away. Charles now sees that many foster homes have disingenuous intentions with these vulnerable children.

"A lot of the homes that I went [back] to, actually later on. When I went over my records, I went back to find these places. A lot of these places have been later shut down because of health reasons, beating on the children, theft on the children. There's a lot of times when money had been sent to me—it would never get to me, they would use it on their own children, and then leave the foster children pretty much nothing."[43]

---

43 "Homeless Youth Was in over 25 Foster Care Placements before He Ran Away." Interview by Mark Horvath. Youtube. September 11, 2013. Accessed July 9, 2019. https://www.youtube.com/watch?v=NsA5dvpJYyg.

There are foster homes with genuine intent and ability to help children who desperately need stability and a safe place. But other foster caregivers are ill equipped to serve youth who, because of negative experiences and abuse, are thrust into the court system.

Factors of unstable or dysfunctional home situations, the juvenile system, economic poverty, and residential instability differ from those of adult homelessness. With so little control over their own lives and choices, youth often see no alternative but life on the streets.

# CHOOSING THE STREETS

---

Individuals line up around the block. They are huddled in groups of twos and threes, although there are also many who are alone. The scene is reminiscent of lines for a highly-anticipated concert. People wait all afternoon, tired but looking forward to the warmth and shelter of the indoors, the food and drink.

Only this particular line awaits no concert or show. This straggling line is for a different kind of shelter and the crowd is worn and weary. They come day after day; on good days and bad, during storms and brutal heat. Especially in the dead of winter, crowds line up as soon as the shelter allows in hopes of getting a spot in these overcrowded homeless shelters.

Inside and to the back, sleeping mats are crammed closer than close along the concrete floor in an attempt to make room for the hundred and more seeking a place to sleep. The first individuals to get in usually choose the bunk beds. The top bunk offers a little more privacy. The bottom bunk puts one closer to their belongings.

There is no locker or protected space for a bundle of belongings. Coats might be hung on the rung of a bed frame, other belongings stowed underneath the bottom bunk or along the bed where they can be watched. Only the realistic fear of these transient residents is that each time they leave the room or close their eyes, there's the possibility that clothes, shoes, and scraps of money folded within might be stolen within the blink of an eye by another desperate human.

Sleeping is difficult. Other occupants toss and turn, there is the hoarse sound of intermingling snores from every direction, the crinkling of food packages snuck in and opened, as well as the mutters from sleep-talkers and restless neighbors.

Homeless youth looking for a place to stay could stay in one of these shelters, yet many don't.

**

Rolin is no stranger to homeless shelters. He'd rather spend his nights on the street than claim a bed of his own. As a Sioux City native, he went to jail at age 21 and upon release he wound up in Lincoln, Nebraska, when he followed his mom there for a job. The two shared an apartment together until his mother passed away three months later. He struggled to pay the bills without his mom until he was evicted. He has been on the streets ever since. Rolin does not stay at the nearby shelter even though it is less than two blocks away and almost always has open beds.

"The back [of the shelter] is a blackzone, there's no security cameras. Anything can happen back there."

There are institutions that offer shelter only to exacerbate issues such as stealing and harassment, given the close living quarters. Rolin reported the local shelter does not separate the sleeping quarters by demographics such as age or gender. Because of that, many homeless choose to stay in the streets over going to shelters, even when the weather turns bitterly cold and they risk hypothermia or death.

\*\*

David was previously homeless due to his mental illness, schizophrenia, which went untreated until he was arrested on the streets and the courts realized he was in need of help.

David was able to turn his situation around and thereafter became an advocate for the homeless and those with mental illness. His time without permanent housing taught him a lot about the dangers of shelters and the reasons why some homeless choose to avoid them, even in dire, life-threatening situations. In an interview with NPR he gave his side of what his experience was like surviving as a homeless person in Washington D.C. where the coldest nights can drop to zero degrees Fahrenheit.[44]

"All I can say is that my fear of the unknown, of what might be waiting for me at that shelter, was worse than my fear of the known risk, you know, of staying out on the street. That was where I was comfortable. And I think people, we're creatures of habit. We get comfortable in the most uncomfortable positions, and that just becomes home."

Rather than sleeping where the cold could not touch him, David and many other homeless make the choice every winter to endure the freezing winter nights and the fears that come with it. Their fear of what could happen to them in the shelters outweighing the very real threat of hypothermia and death.

---

44  "Why Some Homeless Choose the Streets Over Shelters." Interview. *Talk of the Nation* (audio blog), December 6, 2012. https://www.npr.org/2012/12/06/166666265/why-some-homeless-choose-the-streets-over-shelters.

"Well, not being in a shelter during the coldest nights is just, you know, fear of not waking up in the morning. It's fear of freezing to death. But you learn how to adapt. You learn how to, you know, stuff newspapers in your clothing to keep warm. You learn about hypothermia vans that come by and pass out blankets. And I found it a lot easier to deal with [the cold] eventually than the heat in the summer."

There were times David stayed in the shelters during the period he was homeless.

"I spent most of my time homeless out on the street. It wasn't until the very end of my homelessness that I ended up in a shelter. And I found out that a lot of what I was afraid of was true. I never found out what a body louse was until I got into the shelter. You know, I had my shoes stolen, just like people said you get your shoes stolen, although I will say that there were three people in the shelter who offered to give me a pair of shoes after that happened.

So, there is a sense of community there. I don't want to give the impression that everyone in the shelter is bad. But you have a lot of people with a lot of problems, and so when you cram them all together, you just have one big problem. That's why I'm a big fan of scattered, smaller-sized shelters, where people can get more focus on what they need to get help."

The issues the adult male population faces in shelters—of health and safety—are compounded when the individual seeking shelter is under-aged.

**

Samantha Batko, a prominent research associate at the Urban Institute in the homeless field, said in her interview with *Youth Today*, "There is not enough dedicated youth shelter space, and youths may not enter adult shelters out of fear and they may feel uncomfortable with older adults."[45]

Many youths do not feel safe in the same shelter as adults. No matter how well-intentioned the staff is, the shelter can turn into hunting grounds for predators seeking vulnerable occupants. Contrary to the belief that homeless shelters are safer than sleeping outside, many homeless youth would attest to the opposite. Often, predators trail youth who are on the way to enter or exit a homeless shelter and then assault the victim. Shelters may not have the proper equipment to monitor all areas of the living spaces at all times and often the staff is not trained to handle violent situations, nor are they expected to put themselves in danger.

---

45 Glier, Ray. "The Problem of Youth Homelessness Is Not the Fault of the Youth, Experts Say." Youth Today. February 22, 2019. https://youthtoday.org/2019/02/the-problem-of-youth-homelessness-is-not-the-fault-of-the-youth-experts-say/.

Previously homeless youth Kylyssa Shay said, "Once you get raped or assaulted in a shelter or because you were trailed after leaving one, you just don't want to try it again, no matter how hot or cold or rainy or otherwise unpleasant it is outside."[46]

There are other reasons youth may avoid staying at shelters. Those who choose to sleep 'in the rough,' or outside, may have a fear of contracting parasites. Previous occupants in a shelter's bed frequently bring in different types of body louse with them such as bedbugs, lice, crabs, scabies, and more. No matter how many fresh sheets are brought in, when beds are interchanging occupants on a nightly basis the mattresses harbor the ailments of past residents and the odds of getting infested are much higher. The outdoors may have ants, crickets, and other small bugs to deal with, but some homeless consider them a small nuisance compared to what infested shelters dole out.

---

46  Shay, Kylyssa. "Why Don't Homeless People Use Shelters?" Soapboxie. January 27, 2017. https://soapboxie.com/social-issues/why_homeless_people_avoid_shelters.

Often, shelters have rules against pets as well. A beloved pet may be the only steady companion homeless youth have on the streets and leaving them outside alone isn't an option. When the choice is between giving up a beloved companion or having a place to stay for a few nights, it is no wonder so many choose the first.

Another very real concern is discrimination. While many would like to believe LGBTQA discrimination is a thing of the past—that is not the reality at some homeless shelters. It is estimated that 40 percent of homeless youth identify as LGBTQA while only 7 percent of the general youth population do.[47]

There is widespread discrimination at many of these federally funded organizations that can make the search for a place to stay even more devastating for youth fleeing from homes that are unaccepting of their LGBTQA identities.

---

47  "Our Issue." True Colors United.

The young and homeless are less likely to seek institutional shelters, having heard stories of what could potentially happen to them there. The fear of rape and predatory behavior, the possibility of having one's possessions stolen, the chance of body louse, and the higher incident of discrimination make shelters for the youth an unlikely choice when they find themselves on the streets. That being the case, they suffer the elements as best they can as they look for other options to survive.

# THE DEGREE
# DIFFERENCE

———

A common saying among college professors is that for every hour you put in class you should be spending three hours outside of it working on homework and studying. The average course-load for students is 15 credits a semester, or about one hour per credit for a grand total of 45 hours studying plus 15 hours in class which equals 60 hours. Being a student is a full-time job, plus overtime by this metric. And that does not even begin to cover the extra time students put into extracurriculars, such as campus involvement, Greek life, clubs, volunteering, part-time jobs, and somewhere in there, having a personal life.

For the young and homeless aspiring for a high school and a college diploma, the workload is even more. They must juggle all the above, while constantly dealing with the overwhelming thoughts of, 'where am I going to get my next meal,' and 'where can I sleep tonight.' Whether they are pursuing their GED, high school diploma, or higher education, the actual process of accomplishing this goal is a miraculous feat with implications most people cannot begin to imagine.

## YOUTH AND EDUCATION

Earl J. Edwards was a formerly homeless high schooler who became a teacher later in life. His experiences gave him the unique perspective to know what it feels like to be both the student in homeless situations and later, the teacher wanting to help, and to understand what communication problems arise.[48]

> *"In the middle of my freshman year of high school, I started my fourth episode of homelessness. My parents, five brothers, and I migrated back and forth from relatives' living rooms, motels, and family shelters for more than two years. By the time I graduated from high school, I had moved a total of 14 times."*

48  Edwards, Earl J. "Advice from a Formerly Homeless Youth." Education Week. February 20, 2019. Accessed July 09, 2019. https://www.edweek.org/ew/articles/2017/04/18/i-was-a-homeless-student-and-invisible.html.

The homeless population's relationship with constant mobility is part of what makes it so difficult for the youths to stay enrolled and attend the same school. It also makes constant attendance a hard feat to achieve. Youth and families are more preoccupied with meeting their immediate needs rather than the pursuit of an education. Homeless students have to juggle barriers such as lack of transportation to school, no money for school supplies, fatigue and hunger, and lack of information on programs available, given their situations. These barriers result in decreased enrollment and attendance. Approximately 87 percent of homeless youth are enrolled in school, while only 77 percent are regularly attending.[49]

Changing schools can have a negative effect on a student's social and academic well-being, leading to lower scores on tests and poorer academic performance according to many studies.[50]

An overcrowded living situation is also detrimental to student performance. Whether its multiple families living in a housing unit made for only a few people, or shelters stacked full, these types of living situations produce anxiety and stress.

---

49  "Education of Homeless Children and Youth." National Coalition for the Homeless, September 2009. https://www.nationalhomeless. org/factsheets/education.html#footnotes).

50  Duffield, Barbara, Patricia Julianelle, and Michael Santos. *The Most Frequently Asked Questions on the Education Rights of Children and Youth in Homeless Situations*. Report. September 2016. http://nlchp. org/wp-content/uploads/2018/10/McKinney-Vento_FAQs.pdf.

Common sense suggests it is harder to study or focus in areas with a lot of activity going on, such as chatter, playing, fights, and family spats. As well, the younger or endangered youth cannot leave unaccompanied so studying in these situations or not at all is their only choice.

A study by Chapin Hall reported that one in thirty youths ages 13–17 experience some form of unaccompanied homelessness throughout the course of a year. This means one student in the average classroom size is dealing not only with the pressures of juggling grades, attendance, extracurriculars, and all the anxiety of growing up and being a normal kid, but with trying to meet basic needs every evening such as food and safety, and finding a place to sleep.[51]

> *"Although my parents notified my school district of when we became homeless, I was unaware that anyone knew of our circumstances," Edwards goes on. "I never spoke to any teachers, counselors, or administrators about my living conditions, and no one ever asked me about them. Keeping such a secret was extremely difficult, but fear of being reported to the Department of Social Services kept me silent. I spent more energy*

---

51 Morton, M.H., A. Dworsky, and G.M. Samuels. *Missed Opportunities: Youth Homelessness in America.* Report. Chapin Hall, University of Chicago. November 2011. http://voicesofyouthcount.org/wp-content/uploads/2017/11/ChapinHall_VoYC_NationalReport_Final.pdf.

*lying about where I lived than studying, and as a result*
*my grades dropped dramatically."*

Often these students are not getting physical, emotional, and basic needs met at home. They may want or need guidance from a mentor at school, but don't know how to communicate it or may be afraid or embarrassed of discussing their situation.

"*As a student experiencing homelessness, I wanted my teachers to attend to my social and emotional needs. But now, as a former high school and special education teacher myself, I understand why my teachers did not respond to my needs: They did not know. As a teacher, I never received training on the McKinney-Vento Act, nor was I informed that there were homeless youth at my school. The McKinney-Vento Act requires state coordinators to train district liaisons on identifying homeless students and implementing the policy. Each district liaison is then charged with disseminating the information to his or her respective school leaders and supporting the homeless youths identified. Teachers are not mandated to learn about the McKinney-Vento Act. Thus, many teachers are often uninformed about homeless populations at their school," said Edwards.*

The McKinney-Vento Act is a comprehensive piece of legislation that was signed into law in 1987. The original version consisted of 15 programs that were either created or reauthorized by the act. Through an array of federal agencies, it provides a spectrum of services for the homeless, including in the area of education.[52]

The McKinney-Vento Act defines homelessness regarding the young as, 'children and youths who lack a fixed, regular, and adequate nighttime residence.' Through the Education for Homeless Children and Youth (EHCY) program, the Act aids state educational agencies (SEAs) in providing grants to local education agencies (LEA) to ensure that all homeless children and youth have equal access to the same free, appropriate public education.[53]

LEAs use their funds for activities such as tutoring, supplemental instruction, and referral services for homeless children and youth as well as provide for a liaison at the local level for families experiencing homelessness. These liaisons must ensure that homeless youths and children are identified and enrolled in school, that the school personnel receive professional development and support, and ensure

---

52  "Homelessness: Targeted Federal Programs." *Homelessness: Targeted Federal Programs.* Federation of American Scientists, October 18, 2018. https://fas.org/sgp/crs/misc/RL30442.pdf.

53  Ibid.

that homeless children, youth, and families receive referrals to health, dental, mental health, housing, substance abuse, and other appropriate services. It is also the liaison's duty to ensure unaccompanied youth are informed of their status to receive financial aid support for college.[54]

Notably, according to the McKinney-Vento Act, homeless youth can remain at their school of origin during their duration of homelessness, and until the end of the academic year in which they are able to finally obtain housing. School of origin is defined as the school the student last attended or the school at which the student attended last when they last had permanent housing. Staying at the same school is often in the student's best interest as research demonstrates that students who move perform poorer academically and socially. Transportation is also provided to the school, if it is in the student's best interest to remain there.

Unfortunately, the identification of homeless youths is difficult when families and youths don't self-report and teachers are unaware of a student's status. Communication is vital in these situations, but hard to accomplish.

---

54 "McKinney-Vento Act: Two-page Summary." SchoolHouse Connection. August 1, 2018. Accessed July 10, 2019. https://www.schoolhouseconnection.org/mckinney-vento-act-two-page-summary/.

## EMANCIPATION

When parents and family are absent, the unaccompanied youth seeking education may face problems particular to their situation. The legal processes that become involved can prove difficult for the youth. Bobby Berk had this situation arise when he sought to continue public school education as a minor but found out it was not as simple as enrolling.

Berk's relationship with his family was unlike some other runaways in that his parents wanted him to come back. They even used his quest to receive public education at a school in Springfield as a ploy to draw him back home. They used the law on the books in Missouri that stated a student could not enroll in school as a minor without parental consent.

"When I went register myself for school in Springfield, that's actually when my parents tried to use that as an excuse or demand to make me come home. They're like, 'If you want to go to school you have to come home.' Because you have to have your parent's permission to enroll in school. […] so, they wouldn't let me enroll in school," Berk said in his interview with Jonathan Van Ness.[55]

Berk petitioned the court for emancipation. His new legal status would give him the authority to enroll in school. He did

---

55 "What's Your Origin Story? with Bobby Berk." Interview. *Getting Curious with Jonathan Van Ness* (audio blog), July 24, 2018.

not get a lawyer because he could not afford one, although it was still necessary to pay a small filing fee.

Education is key when it comes to paving the path forward out of homelessness and into a more stable, prosperous life. Those who are not able to complete a degree at the high school level are much more likely to struggle to make a living, not find a living wage paying job, and experience chronic homelessness. In fact, youths with less than a high school diploma or GED have a 34.6 percent higher risk of going into homelessness.[56]

## HIGHER EDUCATION

According to college financial aid applications there are around 68,000 homeless youths currently attending college in the United States.[57] Yet, in one of the largest surveys in the Wisconsin area, known as the, '2018 Still Hungry and Homeless in College,' a different picture emerged. Sara Goldrick-Rab, Founder of the Hope Center and Temple University professor's survey incorporated over 43,000 students and 66 institutions. The reported findings were that nearly one in ten college students had been homeless in the last year of

---

56  Morton, M.H., A. Dworsky, and G.M. Samuels. *Missed Opportunities*
57  "Homelessness on Campus." Interview by Lee Cowan. CBS News. January 20, 2019. Accessed July 9, 2019. https://www.cbsnews.com/news/homelessness-on-campus-the-toughest-test-faced-by-tens-of-thousands-of-college-students-in-america/.

2018—they did not know where they would find a place to sleep at least one night.

The report results also showed that 36 percent of respondents considered themselves food-insecure in the 30 days preceding the survey, 36 percent were housing insecure, while 9 percent were considered homeless.[58] Community College students were affected at a disproportionate amount, with 51 percent housing insecure, compared to the previous year's 46 percent.

In an interview with CBS News Goldrick-Rab said, "One of the things that's changed in the United States over time is that, if you grew up without money, we have sent a pretty strong signal to those students that financial aid is available, and you should try college, because it's your route out of poverty."[59]

College opens the door to opportunities in higher paying fields and makes their graduates more competitive than those without the degree. But the barriers to education and resources needed to attend can make it an unsupportable option for those who are struggling to meet basic needs of living, shelter, and food.

---

58  Goldrick-Rab, Sara, Jed Richardson, Joel Schneider, Anthony Hernandez, and Clare Cady. *Still Hungry and Homeless in College*. Report. April 2018. https://hope4college.com/wp-content/uploads/2018/09/Wisconsin-HOPE-Lab-Still-Hungry-and-Homeless.pdf.

59  "Homelessness on Campus." Interview by Lee Cowan.

"It's hard to view [college] as a *problem*. I'd say the problem is that they're going to college, but we didn't build the support for them," Goldrick-Rab said.

Homeless college students have the option of applying for student-loans, financial aid, and scholarships or grants. But unlike K-12 education, much of the federal support programs for colleges are currently non-existent.

A 2019 report found that the average total cost to attend college for public college was $25,290 in-state, $40,940 out of state, and $50,900 for private colleges. This report only included the cost of tuition, and fees such as: transportation, books, and supplies, and room and board. There still remains the hidden fees of food and living expenses.[60]

### BARRIERS TO FINANCIAL AID

Unaccompanied youth do not need a parent signature regarding FAFSA forms. They are considered an independent adult. Yet a GAO report from 2016 found that rules applied to financial aid programs can make it considerably harder for homeless youths to receive financial assistance for

---

60   Miller, Madison. "Average Cost of College in America: 2019 Report." ValuePenguin. April 23, 2019. Accessed July 10, 2019. https://www. valuepenguin.com/student-loans/average-cost-of-college.

higher education, such as requirements verifying the status of the youth.

> *"Unaccompanied homeless youth are required by law to have their status verified by either an official of specified federal homeless programs or a college financial aid administrator each time they apply for federal grants and loans. Obtaining documentation from specified program officials after the first year of college can be difficult because these programs generally do not serve homeless youth throughout college and because Education guidance on the role of these officials is unclear. Further, according to Education officials and other stakeholders, financial aid staff are often reluctant to determine that a student is unaccompanied and homeless without making extensive documentation requests, yet homeless youth living in a car or tent can find it difficult to document these tenuous living situations."*[61]

Foster youths are eligible for an HHS (United Stated Department of Health and Human Services), program to receive vouchers to help pay college expenses. The issue here comes

---

61  *Higher Education: Actions Needed to Improve Access to Federal Financial Assistance for Homeless and Foster Youth.* Report. United States Government Accountability Office. May 2016. https://www. gao.gov/assets/680/677325.pdf.

with age criterion. If a youth enrolls in college past the age of twenty-one, they are no longer eligible for the voucher.

Navigating the financial aid world is complex for these young adults who often have no parental figure to guide them. Although financial information should be accessible to all, it is not tailored to this demographic of our society and can be difficult for them to understand. Often there is even the lack of awareness of options available to them.

**

Alyona was a 19-year-old college student at the time *Invisible People.tv* interviewed her. She had been adopted from Russia. She shared how her parents used to help her pay rent until they were no longer able. Alyona and her boyfriend had plans to move in with a friend until the situation took a horrible turn. All her things were moved into the friend's garage, but then they said she could no longer live there. She never got any of her things back, which were essentially stolen. She and her boyfriend had to start panhandling on the streets while attending college—an unsupportable situation.

"I moved out of my parents' house at eighteen […] I'm going to school as a full-time student. I had like six to seven classes a day." She said, "We're both going to college still. I only have two classes."

The stress associated with housing insecurity can make handling a full course load an impossible feat.

"It's hard to manage thinking, 'where are you going to sleep tonight' to your homework. And going to class, managing your classes, and where you're going to stay tonight. Like last night I slept in a park with two blankets. Very thin blankets. And at nighttime, as hot as it is [during the day] it gets very cool at night."[62]

Given the unique struggles that homeless and housing-insecure individuals seeking education face, it should come as no surprise that the basic needs insecurity can lead to lower academic performance as well as mental health problems such as anxiety and depression, and impaired physical health.[63]

** 

Mary entered the foster care system when she was eleven years old and was a ward of the state until she was seventeen. She transitioned into a homeless college student couch-surfing with her son while maintaining a career as a self-acclaimed entrepreneur and rapper. What pushed her out of

62  "Young Homeless Girl Is a College Student 'flying a Sign' in Pasadena." Interview by Mark Horvath. YouTube. August 20, 2012. https://www.youtube.com/watch?v=VbkhD-srDQ8.
63  Goldrick-Rab, Richardson, Schneider, Hernandez, and Cady. *Still Hungry and Homeless*

her apartment was a grievance with her landlord for two and a half years of negligence of the property. There was a hole in the roof and when it was raining the apartment was, 'Like a swamp.'

She graduated from community college in Philadelphia with a degree in Art and Design. Mary had high honors and was a member of the honors society. She was accepted to all the colleges she applied to including her dream school, NYU's Kanbar Institute of Film and Television. But after all that work, and achieving her dream, she could not accept it.

"Unfortunately, after receiving my financial aid package along with all of the loan money, grants, and scholarships I was awarded I still was unable to cover the cost of tuition."[64]

This devastating situation is common for people in Mary's position. The potential debt associated with student loans make them financially risky for someone who is already homeless. But Mary is not one who gives up easily. She sees value in the education she receives and looks to it as her shot to a better life:

---

64 "Homeless College Student Shares Her Story and Some Hip Hop on Its 44th Anniversary." Interview by Mark Horvath. YouTube. August 11, 2017. https://www.youtube.com/watch?v=JoY25s5LoVQ.

"Education is extremely important because it is one of the only things that can't be taken away from you, you know once you learn something, once you master it, it's with you forever. And it's the only way to get a good job now-a-days."

When one doesn't know where they'll sleep from night to night the challenges of studying and attending school battle against the necessity of living.

"It makes it hard to focus, but I'm driven, so I kind of put that in the back of my mind and just press on. You got to just move forward, and it's extremely tough."

Attending college while struggling with homelessness is a herculean task.

### WINTER BREAK

Traditionally most colleges shut down their dormitories over the winter break and students must evacuate the premises during this several weeklong-span. This long-anticipated school vacation is viewed with anxiety and dread for students who may be just out of the foster care system, on the outs with their parents, or with a family unable to afford housing. The problem this poses for homeless college students is such that they do not have anywhere to live during the coldest part of the year and may fear reaching out to other students, professors, or counselors due to the stigma they fear with homelessness.

There is an increasing awareness among colleges for the need to address these key issues specific to a small portion of their residents. Florida State University has implemented a program called the cohort model. The University picks out first-generation, low-income, or homeless students and watch over them during their time at FSU. When it comes time to figure out which students need extra help during winter break, the administrators should already have the students identified.[65]

Another type of model is known as the service model. Educational institutions incorporating this model take the approach of sponsoring or starting a program to pay for these 'risk' students with year-round housing, including winter break and most of the summer. Kennesaw State University in Georgia incorporates the cost of winter housing into the cost students pay for housing. They have emergency housing apartments set up for those students in need.

---

65  Bauer-Wolf, Jeremy. "Homeless College Students Struggle to Find Lodging, Food over Winter Break." Inside Higher Ed. January 15, 2019. Accessed July 10, 2019. https://www.insidehighered.com/ news/2019/01/15/homeless-college-students-struggle-find-lodging-food-over-winter-break.

Iowa University waives the cost for students unable to pay for housing over break. Their normal charge is $300 for the whole break.

While the goal exists for most universities to help this population, issues arise for those educational institutions who simply cannot afford to let students stay on campus without paying for the attendant costs.

**TAKEAWAYS**

The conundrum for educational institutions is three-fold: that of identifying homeless youths, educating the homeless on their educational options, and finally, in securing the funds to provide for this needy population.

Achieving an education can be extremely difficult for the homeless population. Surprisingly, just living on the streets may not be the biggest deterrent they face. They may be likely facing some type of violence, discrimination, sexual harassment, or living with a mental health illness or addiction.

# IN THE ROUGH

---

## VIOLENCE, EXPLOITATION, AND ABUSE

Many young adults flee to the streets to get away from the domestic abuse they face at home from family and relatives. But without the safety and security that housing provides, they are even more vulnerable to the dangers of the street and ill-intentioned people who take advantage of their exposed and often defenseless situation.

Any discussion of help for this vulnerable population must include the reality of this difficult to address topic. Many homeless youths have experienced physical abuse such as beatings and violence from drunks, strangers, and even acquaintances. Others have been coerced into engaging in sexual acts, sometimes against their will, other times with the promise of shelter, food, or money at the other end. Expecting danger to themselves in the form of acts of brutality and manipulation is the reality for this younger subgroup of the homeless, often with the sense that they have little power to end it.

The grim statistics reveal that one in three youth runaways are forced to perform a sexual act against their will. Youth are seen as easy victims for predators.[66] The exposure these youth have when they are out in the dark, in unregulated areas such as abandoned homes, or in shelters with little security, places them in an environment that those with safety networks of family and four walls do not have to face.

In addition, studies have shown that certain subgroups of the youth homeless population are even more vulnerable to certain kinds of harm than others. The LGBTQA, in particular, experience more violence, sexual exploitation, and abuse than their heterosexual counterparts. Women report higher levels of sexual exploitation than their male counterparts, while they are less likely to be the perpetrators of violence.[67]

---

66  "Substance Use Among Youth Experiencing Homelessness." *Substance Use Among Youth Experiencing Homelessness.* 2nd ed. Vol. 20. Nashville, TN: National Health Care for the Homeless Council, 2016.

67  "Toronto Youth Documents His Life of Homelessness and Addiction | Red Button." Interview. YouTube. August 2, 2017. Accessed July 9, 2019. https://www.youtube.com/watch?v=g4P8PJf4-NY.

People of color are more likely to experience sexual harassment and violence than white people.

## LGBTQA

Youths and young adults who identify as LGBTQA are more likely to be abused out on the streets or in shelters than their heterosexual counterparts in a study conducted by Chapin Hall.[68]

Another study by Chapin Hall found that 38 percent of LGBTQA homeless youths had been forced to have sex, 27 percent had exchanged survival sex for food, housing, or other basic needs, and 62 percent said they'd been abused physically by others.[69] If you are young, homeless, and LGBTQA, the bleak truth is you are even more likely to be physically abused even though often the intent in running was to escape discrimination and violence.

Executive Director Jodi Schwartz heads up LYRIC, a non-profit that serves LGBTQA homeless youths in San Francisco.

---

68  "Behavioral Health among Youth Experiencing Homelessness." *InFocus*3 (October 2015). October 2015. Accessed July 9, 2019.

69  Tarr, Peter. "Homelessness and Mental Illness: A Challenge to Our Society." Brain & Behavior Research Foundation. January 24, 2019. Accessed July 10, 2019. https://www.bbrfoundation.org/blog/homelessness-and-mental-illness-challenge-our-society.

The institution has housed a majority of youths who have been victims of abuse, exploitation, and physical harm.

"It's clear that lack of safe and affordable housing is linked to an increase in exposure to violence," Schwartz said in an interview with *EdSource*. "The institutions that exist to safeguard our community's youth and young adults are failing these young people."[70]

## WOMEN

Young women currently out on the streets may be escaping violent domestic situations at home. They are trapped between returning home, staying in situations of domestic violence, or living in the streets due to the lack of affordable housing options. A Minnesota survey showed that 46 percent of homeless women report they had previously stayed in abusive relationships because they had nowhere else to go.[71]

Due to the abusive and socially distancing nature of a domestically violent relationship, these women often lack the support network that could take them in if they plan on fleeing. Their abusers often use violence as one leg of a strategy to

---

70  Ibid.
71  "Mental Illness." National Institute of Mental Health. February 2019. Accessed July 10, 2019. https://www.nimh.nih.gov/health/statistics/ mental-illness.shtml.

exercise power and control over their partners by isolating them from their support network thereby keeping the victims dependent on them.

These women's risk of repeat victimization when they flee to the streets is high. Research of a set of homeless women reported that thirteen percent had been raped in the past twelve months, and half the women had been raped at least twice at some point.[72] As will be laid out in more detail, many of these women feel no other choice than to engage in unwanted acts, such as survival sex, if they are going to survive on the street. They are in positions where their freedom of choice is compromised, whether by force, physical need, or danger.

Arien lives on the streets of Hollywood. She shared some of the darker truths of being a young, homeless woman trying to make it.[73]

"A lot of the homeless people like me get looked down on a lot. I get guys who try to proposition me with money to go home with them. I get a lot of harassment. I've had soda

---

72  "Homeless Youth & Sexual Violence." National Sexual Violence Resource Center.

73  Kipke, Michele D., Thomas R. Simon, Susanne B. Montgomery, Jennifer B. Unger, and Ellen F. Iversen. "Homeless Youth and Their Exposure to and Involvement in Violence While Living on the Streets." *Journal of Adolescent Health* 20, no. 5 (1997): 360–67. doi:10.1016/s1054–139x(97)00037–2.

thrown on me while I was sleeping one time," said Arien in her interview with *Invisible People*.

## MINORITIES

Young people of color are also more likely to engage in survival sex than their white counterparts.[74] Predators and abusers know that the more vulnerable members of society are less likely to report instances of rape or violence, and if they do, they are less likely to be believed.[75] They may face members of law enforcement who do not take their allegations seriously or find themselves blamed for what happened to them.

Many young people of color report stereotyping or being profiled in the criminal system. There are increased instances of misconduct by police, abuse, and racial profiling toward this group, and in being falsely arrested or detained.

---

74 Dank, Meredith, Jennifer Yahner, Kuniko Madden, Isela Bañuelos, Lilly Yu, Andrea Ritchie, Mitchyll Mora, and Brendan Conner. "Surviving the Streets of New York Experiences of LGBTQ Youth, YMSM, and YWSW Engaged in Survival Sex." *Surviving the Streets of New York Experiences of LGBTQ Youth, YMSM, and YWSW Engaged in Survival Sex*. Urban Institute, February 2015. https://www.urban.org/sites/default/files/publication/42186/2000119-Surviving-the-Streets-of-New-York.pdf.

75 "Voices of Youth Count: Understanding and Ending Youth Homelessness." Chapin Hall. Accessed July 08, 2019. https://www.chapinhall.org/project/voices-of-youth-count/.

Others have experienced inappropriate sexual misconduct at the hands of authorities. The racial bias they face coupled with their vulnerability in the system can make them an easy target for abusers.

In a Youth of Colors Needs Assessment, they conducted study groups where participants related their experiences:

"I was actually 16 and… [the police] stopped me… and searched me. Well, while he was searching me and patting me down, he got a little too comfortable. And I noticed that that happens more often than not," said a female participant.[76]

In short, LBGTQA, women, and minorities, a subset of this already marginalized and vulnerable subgroup of youth homeless, experience a disproportionate amount of oppression and violence.

## SURVIVAL SEX

Survival Sex refers to the practice of selling sex for subsistence means including necessities such as shelter, food, water, drugs, or money. Over a fourth of youth living on the streets

---

76  Jones, Carolyn. "Abuse, Violence Common among LGBT Homeless Youth, Study Finds." EdSource. April 25, 2018. Accessed July 08, 2019. https://edsource.org/2018/abuse-violence-common-among-lgbt-homeless-youth-study-finds/596734.

and about a tenth of youth in shelters have at least one time in their life engaged in survival sex according to a 1999 study.[77]

Of the one in three who traded sex for survival:[78]

- 82 percent traded sex for money
- 48 percent for food or a place to stay
- 22 percent traded sex for drugs

Shockingly, this process of survival sex does not take much time to occur once teens have hit the streets. One in three teens will be lured into prostitution within 48 hours of being on the streets.[79] There was also a strong correlation between this behavior and other high-risk activities including substance use, suicide attempts, STDs, pregnancy, and criminal behavior.

Ka'ek'e lives in St. Paul, Minnesota. She fell into survival sex in exchange for necessities and is familiar with the other risks that come with it, including pregnancy. She has one five-year-old and another baby on the way:

---

77  "Domestic Violence and Homelessness." *Domestic Violence and Homelessness.* ACLU, n.d.

78  "Substance Use Among Youth Experiencing Homelessness." *Substance Use Among Youth Experiencing Homelessness.* 2nd ed. Vol. 20. Nashville, TN: National Health Care for the Homeless Council, 2016.

79  Ibid.

*"You got to sell yourself in order to be able to make it. I don't even know who my baby daddy is. Most of the possibilities are wanna-be drug dealers or gangbangers and they don't want a kid. And I don't believe in abortion so I'm trying to make it on my own."*[80]

Many of these homeless felt that their only choice to survive was to engage in this sort of transaction, especially in the cold winter months, where being outside in subzero temperatures is out of the question. When the stakes are that high, homeless are the most vulnerable to manipulation of people that proffer help, only to then turn around and ask for sexual favors or threaten to kick them out. Sex in these instances is really not a choice, but just what the term implies—survival.

Ka'ek'e had this happen to her when a friend offered her a place to stay and initially only asked for some help with the bills.

*"Who's actually going to actually help you [...] I couch hop, and then it's like, 'oh you can come stay with me just help pay for some bills [and then it turns into] take off your clothes or else you have to leave," she said.*

---

80  Wenzel, S. L., Leake, B. D., & Gelberg, L. (2000). Health of homeless women with recent experience of rape. *Journal of general internal medicine*, 15(4), 265–268. doi:10.1111/j.1525–1497.2000.04269.x

*"And in December it's not so much fun to leave in the middle of the night when it's cold out."*

## HATE CRIMES

Those who engage in hate crimes feel prejudiced against, and safer in engaging in their harmful behavior when their victims lack housing security. There is a lack of empathy among the abusers in these cases. Hate crimes against the homeless in the ten largest cities in the United States rose 12.5 percent in 2017. This was the 4th consecutive increase in the number and the largest amount in over the past decade. The National Coalition for the Homeless in their 2018 report determined that over the past 18 years there have been:[81]

- 1,758 reported acts of violence committed against homeless individuals
- 476 of the victims have lost their lives as a result of the attacks
- Reported violence has occurred in 48 states, Puerto Rico, and Washington, D.C.
- Perpetrators of these attacks were generally male and under the age of thirty.

---

81 "Although Graphic, Arien Shares the Realities of What Women Have to Endure While Living on the Streets." Invisible People. June 17, 2016. Accessed July 08, 2019. https://invisiblepeople.tv/videos/arien-young-homeless-woman-hollywood/.

In addition to hate crimes against the homeless, negative messages by the media play a role in adding to the public's perception that homeless are dangerous, deranged, and deadly.

A series of films called *Bum Fights* instigated a trend of films and copycat films where homeless individuals were victimized in dehumanizing acts such as assault, tying up of a homeless man with duct tape, while others were tied up and thrown in dumpsters, and street fights.

These disturbing media tapes launched a viral pattern of crimes against homeless individuals. Often the perpetrators of the attacks were under the age of eighteen. They treated the homeless as second-class citizens, not worthy of respect or human decency. In one case, four teenagers who were inspired by an online segment set out with filming equipment to a local park. They found a homeless man sleeping in the rough. They tried to force feed him, then set the man on fire. He was found burnt to death, and the four young individuals were charged with murder.[82]

---

82  Edmondson Bauer, Elizabeth, Kris Bein, and Cat Fribley. *College-Aged but On the Streets: Young Adults Who Experience Homelessness and Sexual Violence*. National Sexual Assault Coalition. Resource Sharing Project. May 2017. http://www.resourcesharingproject.org/sites/resourcesharingproject.org/files/YoungAdultsWhoExperienceHomelessnessandSexualViolenceMay2017.pdf.

Despite the prevalence of crimes against the homeless, the FBI does not classify crimes against the homeless as hate crimes. Yet, the characteristics that comprise the homeless as a group—vulnerability, lack of protection from the state, violent crimes because of their status, and negative stereotypes—are the same characteristics found in other protected classes.

The push to classify homeless as a protected class has been up for debate in courts in recent news.

**

## SUBSTANCE ABUSE, ADDICTION, AND MENTAL HEALTH

### SUBSTANCE ABUSE

Whether these young individuals are on the streets due to economic disadvantages, abuse at home, or escaping neglect, they are coping with both the trauma of a past they left behind and the current reality of surviving day-to-day. As a result, many homeless youths turn to substance use as a coping strategy. They use drugs to escape hunger, feeling cold, physical, and mental discomfort, and fear of victimization.

"Since being homeless is traumatic in itself, some of the people that we work with use meth to stay up all night because they're not in a shelter and they don't feel safe when they're on the street all night by themselves. So they use meth to stay alert, or they use heroin to be numb to the scary experience of being outside… Homelessness is itself traumatic, so in an effort to try to cope with that, substances become a part of this maladaptive coping strategy," said Kate Kirkman, the Street RISE Team Lead Clinician at Outside In in Portland, Oregon.[83]

Using and abusing drugs is something that is commonly associated with 'street culture' and widely available to those in the mix. An initial one-time use can quickly become a recurring pattern as these youths struggle not only with their fears of survival but also addiction. While they may be fixing their fears and loneliness in the short-term, they set themselves up to a long-term struggle with deadly substances that take a toll on their health, behavior, and wellbeing.

## ADDICTION

Outright physical harm is not the only type of factor at home that pushes one to the streets, nor is it the only danger

---

83  Lippy, Carrie, Sydney PK, Emily Hsieh, Shannon Perez-Darby, and Connie Burk. "King County Youth of Color Needs Assessment." *King County Youth of Color Needs Assessment*. The NorthWest Network, May 2017. https://static1.squarespace.com/static/566c7f-0c2399a3bdabb57553/t/597fd3ed893fc098807bb872/1501549553222/Youth of Color Needs Assessment_ Final Report.pdf.

a homeless person faces. There is a prevalent relationship between substance abuse, mental health, trauma, and homelessness. A lot of the conflict one perceives due to the conditions of their external environment can happen internally. As a result, unhealthy coping mechanisms can lead to substance abuse and addiction. The homeless, as a community, face deep-rooted mental health problems that may handicap their inner drive and resilience to fight through to a stable living situation.

One such youth, nicknamed Rabbit, is a twenty-three-year-old homeless young man, who struggles with an addiction to fentanyl, opioids, and other drugs. He was given a camera phone to capture a day in his life, revealing the strong pull with drug abuse and what it has done to his life.

> *"I know I'm going to feel sick tomorrow. I don't want to feel sick anymore. It is too hard it's really embarrassing. It's not like I'm alone, I'm at a shelter. You don't want to appear weak at a shelter because kids take advantage of that."*[84]

---

84  Greene, Jody M., Susan T. Ennett, and Christopher L. Ringwalt. *Prevalence and Correlates of Survival Sex Among Runaway and Homeless Youth.* Issue brief. September 1999. https://www.ncbi.nlm.nih.gov/pmc/articles/PMC1508758/pdf/amjph00009-0102.pdf.

Although most of the youths and young adults are not out on the streets because of a drug abuse or substance abuse situation, often they wind up in situations where substance is offered to them. The short-term effects of a high outweigh all the dangers and life damaging effects of tomorrow.

Soon, as in Rabbit's case, the drug use isn't just to achieve that high anymore. The stakes increase in severity as life becomes about avoiding withdrawals. For Rabbit the pain he associates with withdrawal is like a rollercoaster of extreme lows of physical and mental pain to extreme highs.

> *"My use became more rampant and more frequent and because of that my methadone isn't effective. I'm going through withdrawal even though I'm on an opioid. So, I wake up in the morning nauseated, I have cramps, muscle spasms, hallucinations, flashbacks, insomnia, flashbacks, extreme fatigue. If you can think of a symptom it comes with withdrawal."*[85]

Rabbit videotaped himself after picking up a hit and the change in his demeanor was apparent.

> *"I just picked up a use. I went from feeling terrible, irritable, anxious, frustrated to normal, blissful and*

---

85   Ibid.

*happy. I really hope I can find something in life that*
*makes me feel this good. [...] I'm content with every-*
*thing right now."*

But the effects of drugs only last so long. And when drugs turn into addiction, they can influence these children into extremely detrimental decisions such as panhandling for drug money, theft for drugs, and shaping a life where all their thoughts and decisions are based on getting their next hit. In Rabbit's case, he had a chance to reunite with his family but blames himself and his need for drugs for failing to make it happen.

*"[Fentanyl] is the reason I am back on the streets. [...]*
*I ended up stealing all my dad's fentanyl patches and*
*smoked them all knowing that he would go through*
*withdrawal or be in pain from his injuries, but*
*I couldn't help myself. I am mentioning this because*
*I want you guys to kind of grasp what kind of pull*
*addiction has on someone, that they could betray their*
*own father. They gave me a chance to come home after*
*years, and I blew it."*

Drug addiction is a complex issue that is difficult for one person to handle alone. When a youth is in a situation where they do not have a stable household, parental support, or counseling, getting out of a cycle can be next to impossible.

In Rabbit's case, he does not want to be stuck where he is but seeking the help and steps necessary to get out of a situation require resources out there in the first place for the young and homeless.

> *"I don't want to be a career homeless person. I want to have a family. I want to have a partner, I want to have kids, I want to have life. What I have now isn't much of a life."*

**MENTAL HEALTH**

Young individuals are in the stage of life where they are still growing physically, mentally, and emotionally. The brain is not fully developed until the age of 25.

The effects of trauma from homelessness can impact the lives of these youths far into their adult lives. These same young individuals are dealing with a load of risk factors that may include**family conflict, housing and food insecurity, domestic and sexual violence, alcohol or drug use, unemployment, loneliness, stress, and anxiety. It is no wonder that homeless youths are at an increased risk of mental health problems such as anxiety, depression, and post-traumatic stress disorder when compared to their housed peers. Between the ages of 18 and 24, the homeless individual's likelihood of having at least one psychiatric disorder can be four times that of the national average for those in the same age group at 82 percent and 19 percent respectively, according to a report in the *Journal of Adolescent Health*.[86]

While mental health can make it difficult to get out of bed, fulfill requirements to stay in a job, and earn an income, it has been found that mental health issues are often exacerbated by homelessness. Studies show that most people become homeless because of economic and financial issues, not the other way around—that is, that poverty puts these people out on the streets.[87] Once on the streets, mental health is harder to address and often deteriorates.

Young adults aging out of foster care are at risk for homelessness, and may often be waging a long battle with mental health issues. At the same time, they have not had the power or the means to make adult decisions while they've been in the system. Everything, from where they live, to whom they can see, where they go at night, and even such practical skills filing tax returns was handled for them. Part of the reasoning for this is that like any other youth that age, their brains are

---

86 "Pregnant Homeless Girl Talks about "survival Sex" for Homeless Youth." Interview by Mark Horvath. YouTube. September 27, 2010. https://www.youtube.com/watch?v=gFlgirdLiu4.

87 "Vulnerable to Hate: A Survey of Bias-Motivated Violence Against People Experiencing Homelessness in 2016–2017." National Coalition for the Homeless , December 2018. https://nationalhomeless.org/wp-content/uploads/2019/01/hate-crimes-2016–17-final_for-web2.pdf.

still developing, and they are not at the point where they make the smartest choices. Unlike kids in traditional homes, they may struggle with untreated trauma that has affected their mental health and continues to make them act out.

While these youths may be considered old enough to age out of the system, they may not be in a place mentally where they are ready to be let go without help. Aging out of the foster care system or governmental program help may mean the end of treatment for them as they gain their independence and decide not to seek help any longer.

Regardless of initiating factors, individuals living on the street do not have the means to treat their illness. Forms of medicine, therapy, and doctor's appointments are all costly endeavors. It is not a mental health problem that puts these youths on the streets, yet it is estimated one in five youths aged 13–18 will experience a severe mental disorder at some point during their lives.[88]

In order to provide a path of escape from homelessness, it is necessary to understand what factors not only lead youths to fall into the life of living in the rough but what continued

---

88  Marks, Kathy. "Australian Teenagers Filmed Themselves Set-
    ting Fire to Homeless Man." NZ Herald. NZ Herald, Septem-
    ber 18, 2017. https://www.nzherald.co.nz/world/news/article.
    cfm?c_id=2&objectid=3579533.

trauma they are susceptible to once there. It is not a pretty picture to envision. The cruelties life has handed these people take more than a day, month, or even a year to work through. It takes devoted teams composed of therapists, case workers, and mental health experts with patience, determination, and adaptability to work through complex issues that can cause someone to act out over and over as a form of coping mechanism. And an understanding that youth homelessness requires new pathways than what currently exist for adults who are homeless.

# YOUTH CENTERED
# SHELTERS

———

Given the dangers adult shelters pose for youth and young
adults they often have no other choice besides the streets.
Young adults aged 18–24 are often no longer eligible for
family shelters, yet are still at a critical period whereby
many developmental measurements—such as physically
and mentally—they are not truly adults. As discussed in,
'Choosing the Streets,' they fear putting themselves in a vulnerable position at shelters that have been known to be
hunting grounds for predators, their own discomfort level
around adult occupants, and the unsanitary conditions of
the sleeping quarters.

One solution put forward to deal with the problem are shelters made specifically for youth and young adults. These shelters address the problems apparent with adult shelters of safety and sanitary living conditions. Although not yet a widespread concept, shelters such as Y2Y Harvard Square in Boston, Massachusetts, and Covenant House have been ahead of the curve in starting shelters around the US that provide youths and young adults a safe place to check into while they figure out their long-term housing plan.

## Y2Y HARVARD SQUARE

Y2Y Harvard Square is one of the shelters specifically targeting youth populations as an alternative to regular homeless shelters. They serve young adults ages 18–24. Located in Boston, Massachusetts, Y2Y, a homeless shelter for youths and created by youths, hopes to address the needs specific to youths and young adults.

The founders, Sarah Rosenkrantz and Sam Greenberg, created the shelter, and opened its doors in December 2015. The idea started when they were both working at a Harvard Square Homeless Shelter and noticed the increased volume of younger homeless and their unique concerns with adult shelters. They wanted to create an atmosphere cognizant of youth's different physical, mental, and developmental needs.

"Sam and I, the co-founders, were volunteering at the Harvard Career Homeless Shelter, which is a program of PBHA and an adult shelter. While we were there there were a lot more young people coming through the doors, a lot of young people in teens and ages 19 to 20. We heard from them over and over that they did not feel safe in adult shelters and that the housing or homeless shelter was the only shelter that they felt safe," said Sarah Rosenkrantz.

From there, the two started the project of developing and launching a space designed specifically for young adults. They worked as student volunteers at the student-run Harvard Square Homeless Shelter (HSHS). Both HSHS and Y2Y are programs of the larger Philips Brooks House Association, a Harvard College-affiliated group that works to serve the communities in Cambridge and Boston.

"Everything was a key decision, from locating the space, to the physical design, to the program model. I think the first and most important thing that we did was develop an incredible community of supportive advisors. So, we had a really robust community advisory board that included service providers, young people with experience, faith leaders, and academics. Those people helped steer us towards the right resources and asking the right questions. Ultimately, it was that broader group that really made decisions about all aspects of the programming," said Rosenkrantz.

They attribute part of their success with designing the shelter to the time they took in researching well-founded practices in solving youth homelessness, as well as asking the right people what works. In this case, the right people included not only academics and experts but with the young adults who had real experience of living in the rough. Y2Y has a youth advisory board that handles the decisions from policies and regulations to what furniture is used at the shelter. It was designed by young people, for young people.

"What's unique about the design process is that so much of the program was designed by young people with experience. So, for every decision point we not only gathered research on best practices [and] talked to countless agencies across the country doing similar work, but ultimately worked with young people to define what would be the most appropriate decision. So, for example, in designing the physical space, we wanted the space to be fully gender inclusive, private, and feel non-institutional. And so, I think that really sets us apart."

Y2Y's design process is reflected in its five principles of safety, dignity, adaptability, collaboration, and affirmation. The principle of safety is about creating a safe atmosphere both physically and mentally. Like the approach in their design of finding the best resources, collaboration refers to their continued effort to connect with the environment and community to provide the best resources. And affirmation means that this is a shelter that does not discriminate in whom they serve.

One of the most distinguishing factors is that the shelter is run by the youths. They are all young adults themselves and include a mixture of college and graduate students. Many are Harvard students and nearly every one of the staff serve as volunteers.

"We learned that young adults don't feel safe in adult shelters. They are not built to meet the needs of a young adult population. Young people, specifically between the ages of 18 and 24, are very different and have very different needs; developmentally, emotionally, physically, so it was important for us to create a space that was designed and driven by young people," Rosenkrantz said in her PBHA interview.[89]

Although having the shelter run by young adults around the same age isn't a necessity, it certainly has its benefits.

---

89  "The Homeless Shelter for Young People, By Young People." Interview. Philips Brooks House Association. February 1, 2019. Accessed July 11, 2019. http://pbha.org/stories/watch-pbhas-y2y-harvard-square-the-homeless-shelter-for-young-people-by-young-people/.

"Now, I think the biggest thing that we found is that because the people who are homeless have such histories of trauma with adults or kind of an older population, that having a space that's run by young people automatically creates a space that feels that there's trust, and there's a connection. People who look like them and have similar backgrounds and can really relate makes them feel much safer."

Photograph by Ari Daniel[90]

Today, the brightly lit interior of the shelter is painted in shades of lime green and sky blue. Each bunk bed contains its own shelving unit located inside. Overall, the building is more reminiscent of a modern, youth hostel rather than what is imagined when one pictures a homeless shelter.

---

90  Daniel, Ari. Photograph. *NPR*. NPR, January 6, 2016. https://www.npr.org/2016/01/06/461416400/temporary-housing-for-young-people-by-young-people#mainContent.

The shelter, which fits twenty-seven occupants at any time, creates a tight-knit family feel and as one occupant puts it, "I like it here because it's like a little group, a little crew, a little family."[91]

With so few shelters like this, the demand is much higher than the supply. To decide which young adults are allowed to stay at the hostel, the Y2Y does a daily lottery. Twenty-two of their beds are for thirty-day stays while the other five are for one-night stays.

Once a resident, the occupants are offered a wide range of services including medical care, legal services, case management, and even yoga and art workshops. They can be linked up with case management workers and be given information for other programs outside the shelter.

"A lot of people think that anyone who experiences homelessness are experiencing it for some personal fault of their own. It's really so much more complicated. Their homelessness is something they are experiencing, but it's not their identity," said Rosenkrantz in a video interview.[92]

---

91  "The Homeless Shelter for Young People, By Young People." Interview. Philips Brooks House Association. February 1, 2019. Accessed July 11, 2019. http://pbha.org/stories/watch-pbhas-y2y-harvard-square-the-homeless-shelter-for-young-people-by-young-people/.
92  Ibid.

Covenant House is another organization focusing on youth needs. Their youth shelters have roots in over thirty cities and offer housing and support services to a broad range of youths. Not only those under 18 but young adults that have aged out of juvenile services, foster care, been victims of abusive homes, human trafficking, and exploitation.[93] Their youth shelters are part of the second step in a model to provide youths with longer term, permanent care. The first step involves street outreach where they engage the youths who have not found shelter in hopes of providing them with no-barrier, safe, and short-term housing to meet their immediate needs.

This short-term housing is part of their crisis care unit. The youths and young adults who come to them do not have to go through any official channel, and they can come any time of day or night. During Covenant House's intake process, a youth meets with a counselor and have their basic and immediate needs assessed. They are provided with a meal, hot shower, and any emergency medical care needed. Medical assistance also addresses mental health as they are given the psychiatric care they may so desperately need. Their next step involves legal aid, if needed. Legal aid processes may include getting a restraining order, identity change to

---

93  "About Covenant House." About Covenant House. Accessed July 11, 2019. https://www.covenanthouse.org/homeless-charity.

protect from a predator, or continuing to resolve ongoing legal battles.

> *In the documentary, Shelter, one of the employees of the Covenant House in New York said, "So, we get a lot of kids. They're hurt. They've got abandonment issues. They meet each other here. [..] But you know, we've got to love them, we've got to protect them, we've just got to have unconditional love for them, and that's all it is."*

The average length of stay at the crisis shelter is less than thirty days. And each person who comes to stay is unique.

> *"Every child can leave Covenant House and come back voluntarily, as many times as they need. We know many kids need more than one chance to achieve a future free from homelessness – and that is exactly what we provide. For the children who choose to stay with our program, we develop individual case plans tailored to their specific needs so they can begin the next steps in the Continuum of Care."*[94]

---

94  "Crisis Care for Homeless Youth." Covenant House. Covenant House, n.d.

Once these young adults have received emergency services and help with their immediate needs, the ideal next step for them is to transition from the shelter into more stable forms of housing and programs that can help them tackle the long-lasting problems they may experience.

## BENEFITS OF YOUTH HOMELESS SHELTERS

As a form of immediate shelter and protection, having homeless shelters that are geared for youth save them from the trauma of choosing between sleeping on a street corner or an adult shelter where they feel unsafe. In addition, these youth shelters may provide targeted services that are differentiated to a young adult's specific needs, such as help with continued education, mental health services for adolescents, and a sense of community. Elements which can be key to the young adult's developmental phase.

During their time in this type of youth-centered shelter young adults have a chance to get back on their feet and be connected to programs and living services that are longer-lasting. Models, such as Covenant House, offer transitional programs for youth to get involved in their continuum of care.

These youth-centered shelters have stepped into a gap of need for youths and young adults, because there are times when there can be too much red tape and paperwork involved with getting someone housed for a longer duration than a couple weeks or months. Emergency shelters designated for youths are a necessity for people who need safe housing immediately.

# TRANSITION
# HOUSING MODELS

———

Transition housing model solutions are not permanent households for the homeless. They are meant to serve in that interim time-period between homelessness and permanent housing. A place to live while the resident gets back on their feet and learn the skills necessary to provide for themselves and sustain permanent housing.

Transition housing is typically defined as three-months to three-year housing. It is the bridge between a shelter and permanent housing programs in length but provides many of the same services as intensive permanent housing programs that may include supervision, case worker support, and health care.

For youth and young adults, much of their vulnerability with the housing system comes from being at an age where they are still expected to be attaining the skills and education necessary to obtain a job and a living wage. Transitional housing can lift the burden from youth during this critical phase of their lives and make it possible for them to focus on attaining a degree or finding a job.

Research on transitional living programs has shown that there are a few elements that should be emphasized to successfully run a program. These characteristics include:[95]

- Centering the project on the needs of adolescents and young adults.
- Young people must demonstrate a desire for change.
- Adopting a client-centered case-management approach and ensuring that young people have access to a range of services (which can be delivered internally or external to the organization).
- Allowing young people up to the age of twenty-five to stay as long as they need. Young people should not be discharged into homelessness–or prematurely into independent living–because of defined tenancy limits.
- Clear plans should be developed and implemented that support transitions to independent living and adulthood.

---

95  "Foyers." Foyers | The Homeless Hub. Canadian Observatory on Homelessness.

- Focus on personal development, life skills, and enhancing self-esteem through supportive client/staff relationships.
- Facilitating opportunities for youth engagement–with their community and with recreational activities.
- Providing smaller facilities, or scattered site approaches that move away from more 'institutional' settings.
- Enabling financial support where necessary, so young people do not have to pay more than 30 percent of their income on rent.
- Education and training opportunities should be a central focus.
- Aftercare supports should be in place for when young people leave transitional housing.

**YES OMAHA**

YES Omaha, or Youth Emergency Services Omaha, is one of those organizations that offers transitional living programs for youth. The Transitional Living Program is available to youths aged 16 to 21. The residents live in apartment style complexes for up to eighteen months and work closely with caseworkers to accomplish several goals. The transitional living offers supervised housing, life skills training, mental health counseling, medical screening and referrals, and case management. Cindy Goodin is the Director of Programming at YES.

"The youth create their own goals. Who better to tell us what they want? So, if their goal is to buy a car, or finish their

GED or get into college, etc. We help them figure out their path," said Cindy Goodin, "These youth are not unique. They are just like everyone else. They have the same hopes and dreams. They may be coming from a bad situation that they may have no fault in, but they do not have the supports that they need to succeed, so they come to YES, and we assist them in achieving their goals."

To be eligible for the program, the participant must be between the ages of 16 to 21, and homeless. If they are younger than nineteen, they must be either legally emancipated or have their parent or guardian's consent. They must be committed to be actively involved in the program and willing to work or attend school and be involved in the community.

"We have a variety of housing options to fit the needs of the young people. We reserve 2 beds in our emergency shelter that has 24-hour staff for youth who may need more structure or support. We have three furnished 2-bedroom apartments, we have two 3-bedroom houses as well. We also have an extension to the program called Transition in Place, which provides rent assistance and case management for youth in their own apartment wherever they want in the community."

YES also has a program for pregnant and parenting young adults. The Maternity Group Home provides services to runaway and homeless youth who are of the ages of 16 to

21 and are pregnant or parenting. The program is an in-family residency. The residents live there for a maximum of eighteen months and work with caseworkers to solve a variety of goals. They work on many of the same skills and services as the transitional living program in addition to parenting and pregnancy instructions.

"The programs are very similar. The admissions criteria and program fees are the same. The maternity home is communal living. Each participant shares a bedroom with their child/children. We put an emphasis on parenting skills and work with different organizations to help provide parenting coaching."

### THE FOYER MODEL

The Foyer Model falls under the category of transition housing. It's an innovative solution to young adult homelessness due to its focus on the young homeless demographic specifically, case management services, and other types of training to further participant/occupant education and job skills. Originally developed in Europe, it grew in use in Britain and Australia and has since been adapted to serve homeless and aging-out youth in New York City.[96]

---

96   "Promising Strategies to End Youth Homelessness." *Promising Strategies to End Youth Homelessness*. Administration for Children and Families, n.d.

The Foyer Model is different from other transitional programs in that it allows residents up to the age of 25 to stay often and up to as long as they need to. Traditional transitional programs only allow up to around two-year stays. Case managers help youth develop plans on how to live independently and sustainably as they transition into adulthood. Usually the residents enrolled are pursuing education, training, or are already employed. Similar to the Housing First approach, the model enables financial support: young adults do not have to pay more than 30 percent of their income on rent.[97]

As defined by the Foyer Federation, an organization founded in the United Kingdom in 1992, there are three concepts that define the ideology of the foyer model:[98]

- A safe, balanced community of sixteen to twenty-five-year-olds in transition.
- An integrated offer that covers housing, education, employment, and personal development skills.
- A relationship that tailors a, 'something-for-something,' deal between the young person, service, and locality, on which the offer of accommodation depended.

---

97  "Foyers." Foyers | The Homeless Hub. Canadian Observatory on Homelessness.
98  "FOR Youth: Quality Assurance." Transforming opportunities for young people. Foyer Federation.

The Foyer Model is meant to be a solution for the gap that can occur when youth experience a loss in support from parents, foster care, or guardians. Often this happens at the age of legal adulthood. The youth who come to The Foyer are set up with housing for up to two years as well as many beneficial services. It is felt these youth will benefit from a higher sense of companionship and round the clock support.

It is important to note that most of The Foyers require a referral from a local housing authority. The candidate must display a connection to the area, either through a relative living in the area or having lived there themselves for six or more months.

Chloe is a resident at 'The Foyer,' a youth accommodation site set up by the Brophy and Family Youth Services:

"I think that if I wasn't living here my study [at university] would kind of decline, I would be so worried about everything else that's so stressful like making sure that I had food, making sure that I had enough money to live. And just like to pay bills and everything like that. Whereas [staying] here has really relieved a lot of that stress allowing us to get our full potential out of schooling because we're not worried about all of that stuff. They're happy to help," said Chloe.[99] **Citation 4**

---

99  Vimeo. Accessed July 10, 2019. https://vimeo.com/145937823.

## THE CHELSEA FOYER

The Chelsea Foyer at the Christopher in New York City is a supportive housing model that serves 40 young individuals for up to two years. Based on European models, the Chelsea Foyer is one of the first to have been built in the United States.[100]

The Chelsea Foyer project in New York occurred from 2006 to 2013 to compare the results for participants who were placed in the Chelsea Foyer with those were eligible for supportive housing but were not placed there due to the program availability.

Based on the results, Foyer participants had significantly lower rates of shelter use than the comparison group; they were 36 percent less likely to stay in an adult shelter. They were also significantly less likely to go to jail during this time-period at 55 percent less.

The two years post implementing the program, compared to the two years before its startup, saw a 37.6 percent increase in college enrollment and 10.5 percent increase in employment for Foyer residents.[101]

100 "Chelsea Foyer." Good Shepherd Services. Accessed July 10, 2019.
101 "Chelsea Foyer Outcome Study." Chelsea Foyer Outcome Study – CIDI. Accessed July 10, 2019.

**CONVERTIBLE LEASES**

One of the challenges of the transitional housing approach comes with the inevitable move of residence from living in their program apartments with full support to living independently. One innovative solution to this problem has been convertible leases.

Convertible leases offer the option of a slow conversion of the responsibility of the lease from the program facilitators to the tenant. This allows assistance to the young person of not forcing a move if they are not ready or there is not another available housing option of low-enough or manageable price. The tenant still benefits from added support if needed.[102]

**BENEFITS OF TRANSITIONAL LIVING**

As youth and young adults are at a stage of mobility in their life, often the permanent housing that may be ideal for chronically homeless individuals does not apply to this demographic. Ideally, they need a place to live while they further their education, skills, and job possibilities, so that they advance up the ladder of income and educational possibility.

Transitional living is a bridge between shelter life and permanent homes in terms of timeline. Often having some

---

102 "Foyers." Foyers | The Homeless Hub.

permanency in location is necessary for young adults and teens as they need to work on other issues besides housing insecurity, such as family tensions, trauma, and mental health. Transitional living can be a time where these individuals learn coping skills and adult life lessons they may not have been taught previously.

# THE HOUSING
# FIRST MODEL

———

Housing First is an approach to homelessness that seems deceptively simple. It's a consumer driven model that, just like the model's name, is simply—first give people housing. It has seen widespread use with individuals and families spanning old and young and addresses the sub-group of the young adult and homeless population.

One of the primary researchers behind this model is Dr. Sam Tsemberis, a clinical and community psychology practitioner, member of the Department of Psychiatry at Columbia University, and founder and executive director of the organization Pathways to Housing. Dr. Tsemberis and his team first started the research that led to the development of Pathways to Housing and the 'Housing First' approach in the late 1980s when they were running a drop-in center for people experiencing homelessness and mental illness.

As an outreach team, they were trained to identify those homeless who were also having mental health problems and therefore posed a potential risk to themselves or others due to mental illness, because of their location, or judgment. If they determined that somebody was a danger to themselves or others, they would take them to the hospital to treat their condition.

Typically, a trip to the hospital meant an inpatient hospitalization, and some type of medication regimen. The hopes of bringing psychiatric or psychological stability to the homeless person was an emergency room or an 'on the street' type of approach. At the time, the group was not really thinking about housing, or what happened to the person after they were treated. They were dealing with the situation at hand, not the longer-term situation, trying to resolve it in a healthy and helpful way.

This was the approach for three or four years. During that time, Tsemberis and his group noticed a pattern of repetition. During a given year, they would take 300 to 400 people to the hospital, because they met the criteria of homelessness. Typically, they also had some medical problems, mental health and other risk factors. The team determined that about 30 to 40 percent of the people they took to the hospital were returning to the street.

"So, a few months, or sometime later, there was the same person back on the same spot on the street, where we found them. This was what alerted me to the fact that there's something terribly wrong here. Because this isn't helping this person in the long run, we're in this cycle, that is not getting the outcomes we want. The hope was that they go to the hospital, and they would be placed somewhere in a residence or a house of some kind. But that's not what was happening. And so, then the question was, what do we do that's different? Well, what we did that was different was to acknowledge that the approach that we were using was not working.

"You have to be open to looking at what you're doing from the perspective of an evaluation and really being honest, that your efforts are either productive or not productive. And I think we had about 30 percent success, people were getting placed. This was on an early study where we followed people, and they were placed, but at the same time others were still in hospital somewhere. And then of course, the other third was back on the street. That was a very poor outcome. And we were determined to figure out what we could do that was different."

Tsemberis and the team came up with a drastically different approach. It was called a psychiatric rehabilitation rehab approach—essentially an approach used in physical rehabilitation. For example, if someone had a broken leg, you try and help them to walk again. Some people need crutches and others may need a cane, others may need a walker, but you try and figure out from the person's perspective, what it is that would help them the most.

Instead of approaching the individual thinking you're the expert in the situation, you go in as the facilitator of the person's plan. You are not making the plan, instead you are the facilitator helping to enable that person's goal. This new approach incorporated the perspective that the patient may know best what would work for them.

Prior to this the team would talk amongst themselves about treatment options. At some point they would have a little bit of an interview with the person, but the questions revolved around determining illness and if they were in psychiatric trouble. They would ask questions such as: 'do you hear voices? Have you thought about hurting yourself, or have you thought about hurting others?' Most of it pertained to mental health. But with this new approach they wanted to give the individual the opportunity to tell them what was wrong, and how that could be fixed. The change was reflected in the types of questions they were asked. They switched to asking, 'Hey, how are you doing? How are you coping out here? And what could we do to help you?'

"That changed not only the way that we were relating to people, trying to engage them instead of trying to assess them, but it also produced the kinds of answers that were completely surprising in the sense that [before] we approached them as people with mental illness. And now we are approaching them as individuals we want to learn about," said Tsemberis.

The results proved well worth the change in approach. As Tsemberis related, people were remarkably articulate and clear about what they needed.

"I would get responses such as, 'Hey I'm out here, what are my choices, really. I'm afraid to go to a shelter, it doesn't feel safe to me. I've been to a shelter, right? My stuff was stolen, I was beaten up, I'd rather not go to a shelter again. I don't do well in crowds. I'm you know, difficult history, and I don't like people near me," he said.

People would lament that while they were encouraged to go into housing programs, they struggled with the application requirements. Some were asked to take psychiatric medication because of their history, while others were asked to stop drinking beer and be sober for six months before they would give them housing. But, on the street, many of these same individuals shied away from taking medication as it made them feel lethargic in a situation where they needed to be alert and aware of their surroundings at all times. Others struggled with seeing drinking as an immediate problem.

Tsemberis said he remembered getting responses to the no drinking clauses such as, "as far as drinking, that's not a problem. I've been drinking since I was like, 14 years old. I know the difference between, you know, being drunk and not being drunk. That's not my problem it's not drinking, my problem is housing. But these housing people wouldn't let me in unless I could be sober."

Ultimately, the researchers discovered the main thing this group of individuals wanted was a place to live. They wanted something simple, decent, and affordable, a safe and secure place to live. The next step was to figure out how they could provide that as a team of caseworkers, psychologists, and social workers. So, to deliver what people wanted, they created this program.

"Housing First, as the program is called, wasn't called that when we first started. It was named, 'The Program for Individual Preferences for Housing.' That wasn't catchy, but we were trying to be accurate to the term that was actually called the, Consumer Preference Independent Living Model. I was recently at a graduate school and there, it's all about precision. So anyway...we ended up calling it the apartment program, because that's what everybody wanted, not to live in an SRO, or to live in these glue pumps, they just wanted a simple decent place of their own, an apartment of their own."

The group wrote a grant, then submitted it to the State Office of Mental Health. They received news back that they had received federal funding for $500,000. The grant had money for both rent and case management services. It was at this point that the vision and organization, Pathways to Housing came to life. It serves as a nonprofit to bring to life the types of programs the researchers had found successful in their ground-up initiative. They started bringing people right from the streets into an apartment of their own. The organization grew from there. In 1992, Pathways to Housing was founded in New York City. Pathways to Housing trains direct service organizations, conducts their own research policies, and influences policy behind 'Housing First.' [103]

The group realized, based on their treatment, that the rules for other programs that required sobriety or treatment first were completely off base, and stemmed from the fear people would not be able to manage housing.

---

103 "Pathways Housing First." 2019. *Housingfirst*. Accessed October 4. https://www.pathwayshousingfirst.org/.

"We realized that for somebody who had actually been on the street, with the street smarts, and resilience and creativity to be able to survive even a single night on the streets of a city, you know, then surviving in an apartment of their own was a piece of cake. It wasn't somehow obvious until you do it, then of course, it's obvious to everybody. But [at first] that was a surprise. And it was a very pleasant one. And we've just been growing the program since then," said Tsemberis.

**PRINCIPLES BEHIND HOUSING FIRST**

According to HUD, Housing First is based on the perspective that homelessness is first and foremost a housing crisis. To address this issue the priority must rely on providing safe and affordable housing. All homeless individuals can achieve housing stability in permanent housing. Regarding longevity, some people may need support for a long duration while others may only need support for a short time.

Housing First views everyone as 'housing ready.' Regardless of a criminal background, mental illness, or substance abuse, housing is viewed as a human right. In this sense, there are not the prerequisites of sobriety or compliance in treatment to get a place to live. Instead, the homeless providers and programs must be, "consumer ready."

Housing serves as part of a means to an end on improvements in mental health, substance use, employment, education, and general quality of life. People experiencing a lack of housing deserve to be treated with dignity and respect, and should have the right to their own self-determination. The last principle is that figuring out the amount of housing and services needed depends on the needs of the population.[104]

Behind these principles is the idea that Housing First is about what is best for the individual facing homelessness, and how they can be helped. Housing is one of many tools that can be used to achieve the desired results.

"This is often misunderstood about Housing First, because people tend to think about it as about the housing and money, but really, the goal of the program is to have a constructive, helpful relationship with the person, to engage people who are homeless, and to help them leave homelessness and move on to their recovery. Through the relationship, housing is a component of the program so that the service provider of the program has housing as one of the things that they can offer. Just like going back to school or getting a job or reconnecting with family, housing is one of the resources the program offers," said Tsemberis.

---

104 *Housing First in Permanent Supportive Housing.* Issue brief. HUD Exchange.

The focus is the person, because even if the person goes into an apartment and does not do well, it is the relationships that will be there at the end of the day. Typically, fifteen to twenty percent of these individuals need a second or third chance, and some don't succeed even with that. People say they got into an apartment, and then they have had friends still living on the street. They invite their friends over, and the landlord is done with them. They may lose that apartment, but what is key is that they do not lose the relationship with the team. The team is there to pick them back up, help analyze what went wrong, and how that can be prevented in the future. It is all about the continuity of learning and managing the issues of life, and the team is there to provide patience and empathy through these times.

## CORE ELEMENTS OF THE HOUSING FIRST MODEL

### LOW BARRIERS TO ADMISSIONS

The admissions policies are not meant to serve as a deterrent for those who have the biggest disadvantages when it comes to applying for housing such as a low income, unsatisfactory credit score, past evictions, criminal history, or any other barrier. In the case of young adults, this can be beneficial as they are likely to have no credit score or low credit scores and low incomes due to lack of experience. Organizations may choose to award housing based on other factors than 'first come first served,' such as on longevity of homelessness, high levels of vulnerability, risk factor, vulnerability to an early mortality, and other high service needs.

## LOW LEVEL OF PREREQUISITES TO PERMANENT HOUSING

Unlike other models, there is no expectation of completing or enrolling in a program for alcohol or drug treatment, no sobriety demonstration, or agreeing to comply to a treatment regimen to become a participant in the program. Participants are not expected to first enroll into transitional housing or another type of model before entering permanent housing.

As developed by Pathways to Housing, there are two requirements to remain in the program. The first of these is that tenants must pay 30 percent of their income toward the rent. The other 70 percent of their income is free to be used on any other necessities or luxuries the tenant needs or wants. Secondly, the tenant must meet with a staff member at a minimum of twice a month. Both requirements are flexible to the needs of the consumer.[105]

---

105 Tsemberis, Sam, Leyla Gulcur, and Maria Nakae. "Housing First, Consumer Choice, and Harm Reduction for Homeless Individuals with a Dual Diagnosis." American Journal of Public Health. April 2004. Accessed July 10, 2019.

### STREAMLINED ENTRY INTO THE SYSTEM

The housing first model prioritizes a rapid and efficient application and approval process. A lengthy and complicated application process puts undue stress and anxiety on the applicant. Through processes such as consistent identification and engagement with landlords and property owners who have available units, providers can speed up the housing process when it comes to placing individuals.

### VOLUNTARY BUT AVAILABLE SUPPORTIVE SERVICES

Supportive services are offered consistently but not required for the tenant to maintain housing. Services, such as counselors, support staff, and case managers are informed of the philosophy that recognizes drug addiction and alcohol use as a part of the tenants' lives. Tenants are engaged in nonjudgmental communication about these behaviors and offered services to educate and avoid these risky behaviors. They may engage in evidence-based treatments if they choose.[106] These supportive services are also meant to prioritize problem-solving and engagement over therapeutic goals.

---

106 "California Code, Welfare and Institutions Code – WIC § 8255." Findlaw. Accessed July 10, 2019.

## AUTONOMY OF THE TENANT

Tenants are treated with individual freedoms and have full rights, responsibilities, and legal protections. They are informed of their lease terms and have the right to exercise full legal protections in case grievances arise. Just like in a normal landlord-tenant relationship, landlords or providers must adhere to the lease and cannot violate privacy rights or other terms of the lease.

Accommodations are available upon request for people with disabilities within the application and screening process. Building and apartment units include features to accommodate these disabilities.[107]

## POLICIES TO AVOID LEASE EVICTIONS

Although use of substances or alcohol are not considered as lease eviction status by Housing First, the use of illegal substances, selling of, or illegal behavior would all result in lease termination. The team of trained caseworkers, psychologists, and service workers spend time with the individuals so they are aware what type of behavior would lead to an eviction. They take steps to avoid this risky behavior.

---

107 *Housing First Checklist: Assessing Projects and Systems for a Housing First Orientation.* Report. United States Interagency Council on Homelessness. September 2016.

## BENEFITS OF THE MODEL

The model has seen widespread success in both its implementation to differing environments and the outcomes in reduction of homelessness:

- In Utah, the use of this model caused a 91 percent reduction in its rates of chronic homelessness.[108]
- The initial research from the program tracked 139 participants who had dealt with chronic homelessness. In 1997, five years after starting the program, 85 percent of the participants still live in the provided apartments. This is compared to a high of 60 percent retention rate in the next best model programs.[109]
- Permanent Supportive Housing (PSH) has a long-term housing retention rate of up to 98 percent under the Housing First model.[110]

---

108 McEvers, Kelly. "Utah Reduced Chronic Homelessness By 91 Percent; Here's How." NPR. December 10, 2015. Accessed July 10, 2019.

109 National Psychologist Staff. "'Housing First' Reducing Homelessness." The National Psychologist. March 04, 2018. Accessed July 10, 2019.

110 Montgomery, A.E., Hill, L., Kane, V., & Culhane, D. Housing Chronically Homeless Veterans: Evaluating the Efficacy of a Housing First Approach to HUD-VASH. 2013.

- Both PSH and Rapid Rehousing who have consumers in a Housing First model access housing faster[111] and are more likely to remain stably housed.[112]

## GROWING INTEREST IN HOUSING FIRST

The public soon caught on to the success. The federal government tested the model on 734 homeless individuals in 11 different cities. The results came back with health costs nearly cut in half and addiction levels dramatically reduced.[113] This information added to the program's popularity, it is not only beneficial for getting the results, but also the fiscally smart choice.

In Dr. Tsemberis's interview at 'Arrels Fundacio,' in Barcelona, he stated, "One of the reasons I think that the program is being implemented in so many other places is that it turns out that somebody on the street is actually costing the government a lot more money than somebody who is being housed. And I think that governments are becoming aware of this and certainly many of the advocates in every

---

111  Gulcur, L., Stefancic, A., Shinn, M., Tsemberis, S., & Fishcer, S. Housing, Hospitalization, and Cost Outcomes for Homeless Individuals with Psychiatric Disabilities Participating in Continuum of Care and Housing First programs. 2003.

112  Tsemberis, S. & Eisenberg, R. Pathways to Housing: Supported Housing for Street-Dwelling Homeless Individuals with Psychiatric Disabilities. 2000.

113  McCoy, Terrence. "Meet the Outsider Who Accidentally Solved Chronic Homelessness." The Washington Post. May 06, 2015. Accessed July 10, 2019.

community are pointing out that police arrests, shelter days, soup kitchens, many visits to emergency rooms for wounds and other things; when you tally those kinds of things up for some of the individuals in a city, you could be paying hundreds of thousands of euros a year in services like this alone and the person is still homeless on the street, is no better off," said Dr. Tsemberis. "So, this program in the states is somewhere between $14,000 to 22,000 a year and you can pay the rent subsidy and have a case worker that looks after people."[114]

## IMPLEMENTATION OF THE PROGRAM

The program has seen widespread success with over 300 cities worldwide implementing the Housing First model. It has been replicated in large and small cities in America, Europe, Australia, and Canada with more cities jumping on board.

Housing First is a program that was designed to address the most public and hard to solve cases of chronic homelessness in mind. These are individuals who are dealing with mental health issues, substance abuse, alcohol, and addiction. They are the ones visibly on the streets without a support network.

---

114 Tsemberis, Sam. "Interview to Sam Tsemberis, Creator of the Housing First Program in a Community of USA." Interview. YouTube. Accessed January 20, 2017.

The program has seen extreme success, but as Tsemberis relates, it is adaptive to those individuals facing homelessness in any situation.

"The thing that I've learned from this is that, if people with mental health and substance abuse problems can manage an apartment of their own, then everybody else who is just poor, and homeless and in desperate need... of course, can be housed. It would be less expensive, because all they would need is the rent subsidy, not the case management so much, so if you can have the most vulnerable among the homeless, you can certainly house everybody else up the ladder from that, that doesn't have the same level of vulnerability," said Dr. Tsemberis.

The housing first program has seen widespread use in different communities. It continues to grow in use in both urban and rural communities, individuals and families, old and young.

"Our focus has been mostly the individuals but we sometimes house families. But I can tell you that there are lots of programs. There is a Pathways to Housing program in Vermont, for rural Housing First, and there is one in Philly, there's one in DC. There are lots and lots of agencies that operate Housing First programs, and some of them house families. And some families need a little bit of case management. Others, in many cases, just need the rent subsidy, because it's really about poverty. The housing first approach emphasizes self-determination and no prerequisites for housing. Make housing available as a matter of right, a basic human right, like healthcare or education. Which means you don't require people to jump through hoops. You don't require them to be clean and sober. You don't require them to participate in treatment, meet curfews, do everything that the program needs, you give housing as a matter of rights. Then you support whatever else the person needs whether that be finding a job, getting back in touch with their family members that may have been estranged, all kinds of things."

When asked about what a local agency should do if they want to implement a successful 'Housing First' program, Dr. Tsemberis said it is about strategic planning and commitment to the individual.

"I think primarily, it is a matter of commitment the local agency has to, first and foremost, decide that this is what they want to do, they want to operate a housing first program. And then they put their time and resources into getting the kinds of grants and funding to operate the program. They'll need some training on how to do it. But it is not that complex really, it's simpler than it sounds. But really, people just need to make the commitment to want to end homelessness for a particular group of people," said Tsemberis, "Finally don't be discouraged that you can't save everybody, and you're not going to end the whole problem. For every individual you house, that is a life transforming event for that person,"said Tsemberis.

Most importantly is taking that next step to bring the program to a larger scale and show that if supported, it can be successful.

"It continues to demonstrate to the community and to everybody there, that, 'Hey, we can solve this, look at this. We've already solved it for 30 people, 50 people, or however many people it is.' So, let's do more, you know, so it sets something in motion that can be built upon. So, it's very important to us, we start and show that it can be done, and then use that as further advocacy for bringing it to scale," Tsemberis continued.

### APPLYING A YOUTH-CENTRIC FOCUS

Ideally, youths and young adults will not be in programs and models designed for the homeless their entire lives. While the housing first model has permanent residency as an attribute to its design, this feature may not be a necessary feature for programs dedicated to young adults.

Housing first was designed to tackle the toughest chronic cases of homelessness in mind, but the model's attributes are beneficial to a wide-ranging population. Youths and young adults looking for stable housing usually do not have the same preconditions of chronic homelessness as other homeless demographics, but there are still homeless young that struggle with addiction and alcoholism. In these cases, putting them in a housing model that allows them to secure that basic need first, then work on their problems would most likely show more success keeping them housed as the model did for the homeless population as a whole.

# FAMILY INTERVENTION
# MODELS

———

Family intervention strategies are currently three-fold: reunification, prevention, and reconnection. Prevention services are ones that better family functioning and prevent abuse before it happens. These services are aimed at stopping youth runaways before they occur. Reunification strategies are designed to reunite the family with the runaway youths in safe situations, and subsequently lead to the re-housing of youth through these support networks.[115]

## REUNIFICATION

The approach known as family reunification is a client-driven, case management approach. Family reunification is not recommended or possible for those youth who have run away from home that are unsafe due to abuse or lack of support.

The Urban Institute, in their studies of these family intervention methods, noted that approaches that were evidence-informed or evidence-based had several unifying

factors.[116] They were home-based services, meaning they had a home element to them, and services were often delivered in

---

115 *Ending Youth Homelessness Before It Begins: Prevention and Early Intervention Services for Older Adolescents* .Report. July 23, 2009. Accessed July 11, 2019.

116 Pergamit, Michael, Julia Gelatt, Charmaine Runes, and Brandon Stratford. *Implementing Family Interventions for Youth Experiencing or at Risk of Homelessness.* Urban Institute. Urban Institute. November 2016. Accessed July 11, 2019. https://www.urban.org/sites/

a second location in the community or a clinic. All the services involved parent training and clinical services. In these programs, services usually lasted from three to six months, with an average of 12 to 16 sessions. The professionals in charge were graduate-level therapists, and there was often training involved to deliver the intervention, although some staff already had experience.

The key takeaways from their research concluded that there were several factors that could be implemented to make for more successful family intervention results.

The first lesson was to think carefully about how to engage parents. Parents in these situations are often dealing with overwhelming and stressful circumstances. One of the least effective ways to draw them out is through social workers who come across as judgmental and unresponsive to their situation. Social workers should instead work to gain the parents' trust and cooperate with them toward a common goal, rather than against them.

Secondly, incorporate both the youth, the guardians, and their families in the decision-making process. A truly successful intervention requires support from both sides of the aisle. It was also recommended that organizations consider

default/files/implementing-family-interventions-for-youth-experiencing-or-at-risk-of-homelessness.pdf.

a broader definition of family to extend to other members who may play a central role in the youth's network.

Next, for youth and families with complex needs, multiple forms of services can be beneficial. Potential services include case management, clinical services, and parenting training. The setting of the services, whether in the home or a community setting, can be chosen by the family to ensure an environment where they feel more comfortable and freer to engage in communication.

It's also important in family reunification settings to continue to check-in on the family and youth after they have successfully reunified. Many of the currently existing programs offer continued services to the youth after reunification and coaching for the parents. Check-ins via phone call, email, or in person can also be beneficial.

## PREVENTION

In many urban areas, programs for youth become available only after they become homeless. They then move to transition them into housing or provide them with services. Not many have programs for youth and families to help them remain together and to prevent or intervene in early homelessness.

Treatment Foster Care Oregon is a model that addresses problems that could lead to running away and homelessness and prevent it before it occurs.

## DEVELOPMENT OF THE TREATMENT
## FOSTER CARE OREGON MODEL

The Treatment Foster Care Oregon (TFCO), previously known as the Multidimensional Treatment Foster Care, was developed in 1983 after research trials at the Oregon Social Learning Center. Researcher Patty Chamberlain, with the Oregon Social Learning Center, was working closely with youth justice providers and had the opportunity to find a program that would compete as an alternative to residential care and secure custody for young people with serious emotional and behavioral problems, who were also involved with delinquency.

She and her team initiated random control trials. What they looked at was how those young people fared in comparison to their counterparts that went to secure custody or residential treatment. Their study population also had a great deal of homelessness, history of involvement with child welfare, and high levels of trauma. These were often multi-system youth, but through one avenue or another had been bounced into juvenile justice. The outcomes of youth involved with the study program were quite impressive in comparison to the control groups.

The question behind the research was how to better serve these individuals who are ending up in in a variety of settings. The program started with youth involved in the juvenile justice system but expanded later to child welfare and youth coming out of psychiatric care.

"When we examine the youth in the first study, they are highly traumatized, often with multiple system engagement. Although they entered through the juvenile justice system, they often struggled with mental health issues, socio-economic challenges, and parents with limited and inconsistent skills as well as addiction issues." said John Aarons, president of TFCO.

The TFCO model was developed using the theory of social learning. That is, the underlying idea that daily reactions with family and close ones drive behavior that can turn into a pattern.[117] Therefore, reinforcement of negative behavior can lead to a cycle of antisocial behavior. If a child is removed from this negative environment and placed in one where they are consistently reinforced for behavior deemed positive, the cycle can be reversed. Chamberlin continued her research

---

117 "Treatment Foster Care Oregon." Blueprints for Healthy Youth Development. Accessed July 11, 2019.

through conducting eight randomized clinical trials over TFCO and its effects on youth in juvenile justice, mental health, and child welfare systems.

## THE TREATMENT FOSTER CARE OREGON MODEL

TFCO was subsequently developed as the alternative to group care, residential, and institutional placements. The model is tailored to the needs of children, and their program TFCO for adolescents serves youth from the ages of twelve-seventeen. In the context of youth homelessness, the program works as an intervention service.

John Aarons is the president of Treatment Foster Care Consultants, Inc. and currently in charge of Treatment Foster Care Oregon. He has over thirty-five years of experience in the field of juvenile justice as both a practitioner and a leader.

"When you think currently about homelessness, it's sort of terrifying these days, as we have the LGBT community that is poorly served in every system. Their needs do not match up well for[them] to be treated in residential care. It's a group that has higher suicide rates…parents kick them out…[and] in a group care setting, where you add to that the tension and pressure from other young people, which at that age is, of course, a critical influence. Definitely, you see that can lead to these really tragic outcomes," said Aarons.

TFCO is built on the theory that high levels of reinforcement are needed to find substitutes for wanting behaviors and helping to build skills for areas where they were struggling. The program duplicates successful home settings as the environment for treatment. Young people are placed in the home with no other youth in treatment around them. Intensive treatment occurs between the young person, the aftercare, family, and the therapeutic, or foster family, simultaneously.

The typical youth in this program are chronic delinquents. They have an average of thirteen previous offenses and are at the point of removal from their home by juvenile authorities. Often, other home-based interventions have failed for these kids. They may have mental and behavioral problems stemming from deeper incidents that need to be addressed.[118]

Youth who participate in the program stay in the TFCO facility for approximately nine months. They undergo ongoing training, daily support, weekly group meetings, and coaching. The parents receiving coaching on building their relationship with their youth as well as responding to different parenting relationships. The TFCO program emphasizes intensive skill development across multiple disciplines. Simultaneously, for a short period of time, six to nine months, highly supported foster parents live with the youth.

---

118 Ibid.

"This is treatment, not a lifestyle. We want the young person to get in, get out, and get back to life as close to normal as possible," said Aarons.

To create a treatment like this, the program trains and supports the aftercare family and simultaneously works with the young person to give the kind of intensive support that they may not receive in traditional foster care.

The TFCO focuses on five areas:

- A consistent, reinforcing environment with mentoring and encouragement.
- Daily structure with clear expectations and specific consequences.
- A high level of youth supervision.
- Limited access to problem peers along with access to pro-social peers.
- An environment that supports daily school attendance and homework completion.

### DIFFERENCES WITH GROUP CARE

When youth are placed in a group home, incarcerated, or placed in a setting-aside institution, a program is developed to fit over several years and with a large group of people with complex needs. This care is less able to be individualized. In addition, given the settings, there are lots of contact with other delinquent peers. And those

settings don't have parental figures, they have professional staff, so the relationship is different.

There's a great risk of including that population with peers who are delinquent peers, and who are demonstrating other non-wanted behaviors, because then it becomes contagious in the wrong direction and reinforcing unhealthy behaviors. Instead the TFCO approach is to build on positive behavior.

"TFCO is not an alternative to foster care. It is a highly intensive residential treatment. There's one young person, residential level services for one. These are not young people without emotional behavioral problems, they are young people with significant challenges," said Aarons.

One of the benefits of the TFCO program is that it can be individualized. It aims to treat the individual with attention similar to how they would feel in a supportive and safe home. In a supportive home the children grow up with great attention, and they were supported, they were encouraged. They were taught critical basic skills over and over. And many young people don't get those. So, the idea is to replicate that positive home environment.

### FINDING FOSTER CARE PARENTS

The TFCO program approaches finding the right foster parents for their program diligently. In comparison to more traditional foster care, they have a more intensive screening process that feeds into a highly supported training for the people that will have the most direct contact with these kids. Often, when finding foster care parents for the program, the team looks for people who are willing to go above and beyond in supporting their foster child.

"You want people who will challenge the system a little bit. You want people who are willing to be engaged and not happy with the status quo," said Aarons.

The foster care parents go through twenty hours of pre-service training to learn about how the model works. They learn about methods of working with the aftercare family, how to analyze the youth's individual behavior, and the policies of the program.

"These are people who want something different for young people, and they want to be part of that treatment. They are folks who are actively involved in treatment and work closely with the clinical team."

## AFTERCARE FAMILY TRAINING

The aftercare family refers to the family that the youth lives with permanently before and after treatment. This can refer to their biological family, relatives, or a permanent foster family. The aftercare family receives training during the time that the youth is away from home that continues when the youth returns.

The family therapist's sole role is to work with the aftercare family, so the aftercare family learns the same techniques, skills, strategies, and positive reinforcement that the young person is learning, and the therapeutic or foster family is learning at the same time. The aftercare family is getting the same training because so often they have challenges, struggles, and a pattern of behavior that wasn't successful as well.

The aftercare family receives an identified aftercare resource when the young person is placed in a care facility. And then as soon as possible, not only are they learning these new skills with the young person, the aftercare family starts to practice these skills after about the third week. After the young person gets stabilized, they are allowed to start visiting. The first visit with the aftercare family varies from one hour to three hours. From there, they work up to longer stays. During this time the family takes a cognitive behavioral approach into practice. They discuss what the skills they need are and what behaviors are unwanted. The positive skills and behaviors are reinforced through teachings, strategies, and practice at home.

The program has shown positive results in their cost-benefit ratio with a 70 percent chance the program with produce benefits greater than the cost.[119]

## EVIDENCE BEHIND THE MODEL

"There was a study done with the National Institute of Mental Health of young women that were involved in multiple systems. And of course, those young women's instances of trauma are absolutely off the charts. There are disruptions in parenting, parents involved in the criminal justice system, sexual abuse. These young women are much more likely to end up in compromised situations, either in the system or, otherwise, based on their partners, their partner choice. If you can assist them in interrupting that partner choice or getting them out of a compromised situation, the outcome was positive."

What they saw was that these young women—when they were empowered through skill development, through reinforcing many behaviors, through support external to the internal locus of control—was decreased pregnancy rates,

---

119 "Multidimensional Treatment Foster Care." Washington State Institute for Public Policy. December 2018. Accessed July 11, 2019.

six percent lower than the comparison group, and of those that did have children, twenty nine percent lower rate of involvement with child welfare, and a more active choice in long-term planning.[120]6

"I always tell people this statistic is what gets me up in the morning: the number of women engagements in child welfare system was vastly lower than their counterparts who had children. And this is multi-generational families, so the effects are long-lasting," reports Aarons.

Girls who had been through the program were less likely to get pregnant in the post 24 months by 2.44 times. They had reduced rates of self-reported delinquent actions, time spent locked up, and criminal references.

The significant results in the studies were young people who lasted longer in their aftercare placement than their peers. It cured disruptions in the home.

Based on the research, the program has proven to reduce stays in institutional and residential placements, increase attachment, improve brain stress regulatory systems, increase positive academic engagement, and prevent acceleration into youth pregnancy, violence, or delinquent behavior.

---

120 National Institute of Mental Health. "TFCO Model vs Group Home Care Outcomes," n.d.

Twelve months after the baseline, delinquent boys who've been in the program are incarcerated 60 percent fewer days, have fewer subsequent arrests. Two years after, they have less violent offense referrals at 21 percent versus 38 percent of the control group not involved in the program. They also have fewer self-reports of violent offenses with 10.5 incidents for the treatment group verse the 32.6 incidents for the control group. They even ran away three times less often.[121]

"When you're talking about homelessness, they have less suicidal ideation. In addition to that, in terms of well-being and young people who felt better about their lives, there's self-reporting that they feel more optimistic and more able to engage. They saw results that young people were less likely to get incarcerated, to even more likely complete their homework. People start to laugh at that, like, you know, John, in the big scheme of things, come on," said Aarons.

"But if you follow that thread, if they are more likely to complete the homework, they are more likely to then get positive recognition from a teacher. If they get positive recognition from a pro-social adult, they are more likely to respond to that and engage with that and participate positively. If they do that, they are more likely to show up at school. So, I mean, in many ways, it's the whisper that also creates the roar."

---

121 "Treatment Foster Care Oregon." Blueprints for Healthy Youth Development.

"I sometimes say to people, where would you like to be five years from now? Not tomorrow, not next year. As you're thinking about changing systems and improving outcomes for young people it's important to be long-sighted about measuring things over a period of three to five years," said Aarons.

"I always say the goal of leaders when I'm working with them, is to keep everything but the clinical stuff away from the team, really allow the clinical folks to do their work. And you do that by creating an environment where they are not required to do other things that distract them from running the best clinical team."

"One of my favorite things is that clients come in knowing they need to change, even if they're resistant. We tell them, they've heard it and it's not the first time they've heard it. Staff are also more experienced with the need to consider change. Because, you know, that change occurs consistently is the only constant in all of this. Our systems are the slowest, and often most resistant to change," said Aarons.

## RECONNECTION

When reconnecting or reunifying youths and young adults with their families it is important to consider several factors including level of safety, what constitutes the family, and best practice approaches.[122]

Many youths who end up homeless are there because of abuse they have felt at home or lack of support such as in a situation with a pregnant teen or a LGBTQA youth. These home situations may not be safe to return to and are not recommended approaches for this population. A study of 249 homeless youth in Detroit found that of the homeless youth ages 13 to 17, family reunification was a natural outcome for only one-third of the group.[123] One of the first things social workers should check is if the family is not displaying damaging habits and the youth is open to the possibility of return. Reunification may not be possible for youth who do not have extended family connections and be difficult for those who have aged out of foster care, the juvenile jail system, or been homeless on the streets for a significant amount of time.

At the same time when a youth is experiencing conflict with family, often this does not pertain to every family member in their support network. There is often at least one family member present to extend the youth acceptance and a safe place to stay. In today's world, the 'traditional'

---

122 *Family Reconnect: A Path for Youth to Return from Homelessness?* Report.
123 Center for Law and Social Policy. 2003. Leave No Youth Behind: Opportunities to Reach Disconnected Youth, p. 57.

nuclear family composed of a married biological mother, father and children are not the assumed structure. Less than half, at 46 percent, live in a two parent, in their first marriage, structure.[124] Many children live in remarried households, with single parents, cohabitating and not married, or no parents but extended relatives. Speaking to youth on connections they would feel comfortable reaching out to rather than assuming the parents, extends the range of support network available.

## EVA'S INITIATIVES

Eva's Initiatives Family Reconnection Program focuses on getting to the root of the problem at an early stage through counseling. Their counseling revolves around the subjects of family breakdowns, youth and parent conflict, communication difficulties, drug and alcohol use, life and parenting skills, and sibling relationships. Their program offers family and individual counseling to young individuals aged 16–24.

On the site, one youth's story speaks to how he and his mother were saved from the looming possibility of youth homelessness through the Family Reconnection program:

---

124 "The American Family Today." Pew Research Center's Social & Demographic Trends Project. December 17, 2015. Accessed July 11, 2019.

"My 18-year-old son's lack of ambition, drug use, and poor choice of friends were key stressors in our family. I took sleeping pills every night and I cried often. I placed the phone on my bed so I could answer it when, or if, he called at times that he was out all night," his mother said. "Then, through a friend, I learned about the Family Reconnect Program. The counselor asked intelligent questions about the situation and gave me the hope I so desperately needed. I felt a huge weight lifted from my shoulders, having connected with someone who not only seemed to care but who could actually give us some guidance and much-needed support."[125]

Through the support from the counselor, the mother and her son discovered he was dealing with a mental health problem, Asperger's, and that his friend choice was also at the root of the problem.

**TAKEAWAYS**

Whether through prevention, reunification, or reconnection, a successful family intervention can be one of the most powerful and effective tools at preventing future instances of homelessness. Family has the potential to be an invaluable support network through both the structure parental guidance provides and the emotional and psychological

---

125 "What We Do." Eva's Initiatives for Homeless Youth. Accessed July 11, 2019.

needs they help meet for youth and young adults. Of importance is that providers and caretakers should always check with the youth first to see if this is a viable and appropriate solution. Even if immediate family is not an option, there may be connections in other family members worth looking into.

# COMMUNITY
# CHALLENGERS

———

### THE 100-DAY CHALLENGE

The Rapid Results Institute works with communities, organizations, and government agencies to bring about sustainable change.

The 100-Day Challenge approach has had an impact on communities and counties throughout the nation. The relatively new program has housed 3,038 homeless youth to date across the nation.

The 100-Day methodology was conceived by Robert H. Schaffer, owner of Schaffer Consulting in Connecticut.  He was working with businesses and corporations to help them improve their corporate bottom line when he developed this hundred-day approach. His idea is that if you create an urgent crisis type situation, people are more apt to rally around. That sense of an urgent circumstance leads to progress, innovation, and to experimentation.

If there's a crisis, such as when a hurricane happens, all the community will come together and do whatever it takes to rebuild and reconstruct. TSo this was the idea that spawned the Hundred100-Day cChallenge. The hundred days timeline really just provides an urgency to solving a specific time problem. And wWe believe that if you have a shortened kind of time structure, – it unleashes innovation, experimentation, and people are more apt to pick themselves back up when they fail. And so it just creates the container to work with more urgency," said Sean Whitten, sSenior cCatalyst at Rapid Results Institute.

The Rapid Results Institute's founder, Nadim Matta was a partner for Schaffer Consulting. Throughout his life, he had been involved in various types of social impact projects, including nonprofits. Matta was the one who had the idea to take adapt the Rrapid Rresults methodology into for the social sector, to help communities solve social issues that they might be facing. This was initially a branch of Schaffer Consulting, but eventually became its own entity, Rapid Results

Institute. The Rapid Results Institute worked works with a variety of social causes including Justice System rReforms, renovating participation in government, and community development.

The next use of this methodology was targeted for the homeless population. Becky Kanis, previous Executive Director of Community Solutions, whose mission is to end homelessness, read an article about the work that Rapid Results had done overseas. She reached out to Matta and asked if this methodology could be used in the social context of homelessness. The Rapid Results Institute was then invited to work with Kanis's team on a campaign, called the 100,000 Homes Campaign.

A national effort was underway to house 100,000 folks who were experiencing homelessness and The Rapid Results: 100-Day Challenge methodology was introduced into that effort. Thereafter, the methodology was incorporated into the 25 Cities Initiative, which was funded by the Veterans Affairs (VA). The VA chose twenty-five large cities with the aim of ending Veteran and chronic homelessness.

## THE 100-DAY CHALLENGE FOR HOMELESS YOUNG ADULTS

The initiative was deemed successful, and from that point there was a push to connect the methodology with HUD and

A Way Home America in an effort to work with youth and young adult homelessness. The success of this initiative led to parties connecting with HUD and A Way Home America to work on an effort specifically on youth and young adult homelessness.

So far, the 100-Day Challenge has launched six eight cohorts. The first, Jumpstart, involved larger cities including Cleveland, Austin, and Los Angeles. The next three cohorts are HUD 1, HUD 2, and HUD 3, and HUD 4, named after their partnership with the federal Housing and Urban Development. There has also been the Washington State cohort whose aim was to eradicate youth homelessness in different WA counties. Additionally, a statewide initiative was completed in Connecticut, where 7 regions launched 100-Day Challenges in order to build momentum towards their goal to end youth homelessness across the state by 2020. Finally, there is a self-funded cohort whose partnerships are unique for each community.

A key aspect of implementation is the partnerships with the Rapid Results Institution. Each cohort, besides the self-funded, works with specific group partners, such as the US Department of Health and Human Services, Raikes Foundation, HomeBase, Casey Family Program and the US Department of Housing and Urban Development (HUD). The HUD groups are named because of their unique partnership with the HUD who provided the grant. In 2017 the Housing and Urban Development committee invested $33 million into the program. This number was upped to $43 million in 2018.

In the US Senate Report for the FY 2019 HUD appropriations bill, the committee stated:

"By offering local service providers the opportunity to come together to identify impediments and establish goals, the 100-Day Challenge leaves communities better prepared to confront youth homelessness in a comprehensive manner. The program also lays the groundwork for participants seeking to apply for a Youth Homelessness Demonstration Grant award."[126]

## CORE ELEMENTS TO SUCCESS

The Rapid Results Institute grounds its realized success in uniting different branches of the community that specialize in youth homelessness. They bring to the table different providers, government agencies, and even those who have dealt with homelessness first-hand to discuss what would be the best action plan to address youth homelessness in their community.

---

126 S. Rep. No. Committee on Appropriations-115–268 (2019).

"In order for this program to work in the community, there has to be a coalition of the willing. All of the providers and agencies within a community have to believe first and foremost, that they can endure from yesterday, right? People have to believe that it's possible in order to take on a 100 – Dday cChallenge. And aAnother thing that must happen is, communities have to be willing to center this work around youth homelessness. [Those] who have gone through and have lived experience in homelessness, need to be at the table and not just at the table as a representative, but at the table as a core member of the team to help you haveyouth homelessness in their communities." Whitten goes on to say.

Another key element to the program, as discussed in their methodology, is developing a sense of urgency. The Rapid Results Institute creates an environment where the most can be achieved in the shortest amount of time through ambitious goals and a short deadline.

"Instead of a lot of approaches where people kind of sit around and come together once a month to build out a plan, we do that in two days, and then have them enact the entire plan in 100 days. So, there's no community five-year plan to end homelessness or 10-year plan. It's the community's goal and they have 100 days to achieve it. Within that, it breaks down groups of people who may be coming in with badges regarding other agencies. We don't have time for apprehension to play a role, everybody just has to get in there, get their hands dirty and get going," said Whitten.

The Rapid Results Approach is also unique in its take on breaking up power structures and giving a voice to those who normally do not have one in these situations. They ask the people who are normally the ones making all the decisions to step back and let people who are dealing with this issue every day, whether that is because they are taking somebody who's homeless to a doctor's appointment or have personal experience living without secure housing.

"It allows [the young homeless] to have a voice in the best practices and processes that really work. And I think that really changes the dynamic. It adjusts power structures and allows for folks who typically don't have a voice, to have a say, and a choice on what works best for them and the clients they serve," Whitten said.

### THE LAUNCH WORKSHOP

The process of launching the 100-Day Challenge in an area starts with the launch Launch workshopWorkshop. At the Launch workshop, Rapid Results brings the team together for the first time, a team that is usually comprised of frontline staff. These teams include relevant stakeholders from around the community to form teams to represent each city, county, or area.

"We like them to be folks that are closest to the issue, as opposed to just being a bunch of executive directors sitting around the table. We want folks who work with young people experiencing homelessness every day, such as case managers, outreach workers, and clinicians who might have young adults on their caseload for behavioral house, juvenile justice, probation officers and are working with youth that are experiencing homelessness," said Sean.

"We try to take a lot of the decision-making and goal setting to be done by folks who typically don't have a voice in policy and decisions in their community. And of course, young people need to be on that team as well."

That first step brings together all the members selected for a day and a half to two days for The Launch workshop to create one cohesive team. To promote this, Rapid Results have various activities for the members to connect with each other. Then they begin to define what the community issues are and what homelessness looks like for them, so everyone is on the same page. The teams then engage in an activity that begins at the identification of a young person experiencing homelessness.

The goal is to map out the journey for each young person involved, to uncover the pitfalls, challenges, and confusing aspects that young person might experience. This will hopefully set them on the path of determining what will work and what weak spots need additional work. The goal is to do a better job serving the young person in their community.

Once the community teams identified the probable map to attain housing, they then begin to come up with their 100-Day goals. Every community Rapid Results works with must have a number of how many young people they are going to have housed in 100 days.

"We asked them to make it unreasonable but believable. We really want them to push themselves without having all of the data. Like what do you think is an ambitious, audacious goal that you want to set for yourself in 100 days? Because we believe that it's ambitious goals that drive the innovation, experimentation—and that sense of urgency," Whitten related.

This goal setting is one of the core aspects that makes the 100-Day model unique. Part of creating a sense of urgency in the youth homelessness situation involves setting goals that seem lofty to achieve in the set time of one hundred days and require serious mobilization of the community. Almost every community involved sets a steep goal of a certain number of youths they hope to house by the end of the 100-Day challenge. Other main goals range from connecting a percentage of these individuals with education and job opportunities, to the prevention of homelessness for high-risk youth, and creating additional housing opportunities.

"Goal-setting is the hardest part of the Launch Workshop. We always have somebody in the group that's like, 'You know what, let's go low. So, we know we can achieve it.' And then we have somebody else in the group that's like, 'No, let's go really high. Even if we don't make it, at least we're really striving.' So we do [goal-setting] on the end of day one. Just so that way, people can come up with a number and then come back the next morning after having slept on it a bit. Then, you start to see that number increase as they start thinking and brainstorming around. [As they ask] what changes they could begin to put in place in order to achieve their goals. After that, we usually land on a goal they find acceptable," said Whitten.

The finalization of the goals at the end of the day is up to the community teams. On the second day they create their action plans. That is, what are the sub-goals to achieve their action goal? They lay out every single action item to achieve their main goal. For example, one team might decide that by day twenty-five they will find four landlords, or they might start with reaching out to organizations to find identified homeless youth. Each sub-goal entails a specific action with a deadline attached to it and an individual or individuals who are responsible.

"At Launch Workshop where the 100-Day Team set [goals], the tip for knowing when the goal was right is that it should be based on the data and knowledge we have regarding how many youths are currently homeless in the community and be a high enough number to make you nervous or upset your stomach. The pressure of the large goal and the compressed timeframe of 100 days, with the high public visibility and support from coaches, peers, and federal leaders, create the possibility for rapid progress and radical change."[127]

## CATALYSTS

The staff of the Rapid Results are known as Catalysts. What the Catalysts for the Rapid Results Institute do is facilitate the activities and the processes to unleash and bring out the creativity from the team. They are there for support, to facilitate the workshops, and are a link between other resources that they might need. For example, if a group has questions about policy that they need answered by HUD, or if they are curious to know if another community practices shared housing, the Ccatalysts works to find answers to those

---

127  Ukiah Daily Journal. "100 Day Challenge on Youth Homelessness." The Ukiah Daily Journal. August 23, 2018. Accessed July 11, 2019.

questions or link them with the other community to find out how they do it.

## IMPLEMENTATION OF THE MODEL

When it comes to implementing how homeless youth will be housed along with other necessities, there is no set design in place. Each community has the liberty to choose their own course. Housing models created are up to each community and choice is driven by what those resources are. Often communities with youth homelessness have already started to develop strong post-home models and can link homeless to a family that is willing to rent out their room or some other option.

"A lot of times how they implement the model depends on what resources they're currently using such as Rapid Rehousing. Through our process we have them begin to think about, 'Are we using the resources we have efficiently and effectively? And if not, what do we need to do to alter them to reach our ambitious goal?'" said Sean.

The model's adaptability is part of what makes it so effective in every community they go into. The methodology is general enough that it can be applied to a variety of social causes outside of homelessness. With these partnerships the Rapid Results Institution get the expertise needed to mold their program to each specific area and cause. The groups decide for themselves whether to institute models that are permanent or transitional as well as what requirements are needed to be housed. It all depends on what fits the community best.

### AFTER THE 100-DAY CHALLENGE

"What we hope happens [after the challenge is over] is that communities begin to build the muscles to get to a place of irreversible momentum. What we mean by that is that, regardless of any factors, indicators, or difficulties that come up in the community, they begin to build the muscles around collaboration, relationship building, performance increase, and the momentum will continue. For example, a lot of times there's a champion in a community around an issue. And when that person leaves, then the momentum dies. What the 100-Day Challenge hopes to do is allow all of those folks that are sitting around the table to begin to think about this as the new normal, the new way we're going to work. So, when say somebody leaves and somebody else comes in, they rally around that person.That person then understands that this is the way of working in this community to get stuff done." said Sean Whitten.

The communities that have chosen to partner with the Rapid Results Institute on youth homelessness have seen widespread success in accomplishing truly ambitious goals. By learning how to focus their energy and ability to deal with homelessness in such a short timeframe, they gain the perspective of just how much can be accomplished in a short time. The organizations who may not have initially had the right structure and knowledge stream to tackle these issues are left with the tools to now effectively institute changes.

"Organizations that are not set up for success to take on these complex social problems, just because of the way funding streams are from government and state or county, the way data systems are. So, we come in as coaches to help them through this process. You know the work is not done in 100 days. We really think that the end of the 100 days is really just the beginning." reports Meaghan Messner, Catalyst, the Rapid Results Institute.[128]

128 Nouvelle, Chloe. "Allentown's 100-Day Challenge to Combat Homelessness." PBS39 WLVT. February 06, 2019. Accessed July 11, 2019.

# TINY HOMES FOR
# THE HOMELESS

———

**TINY HOMES MOVEMENT**

Tiny houses are fully functional homes built to a maximum size of 300 square feet. This home-owning fad is a popular trend among minimalists and younger generations alike. Relatively inexpensive, they are good for the environment as they reduce your carbon imprint and can be placed on wheels for mobility. These tiny houses offer an alternative to the traditional apartment complex or house and come with the bonus of being both greener and better on the budget.

Most of these tiny homes can be built within a time span of six months. They are seen as unique for their exquisite designs, sustainability, and innovative storage space. They also pose an affordable solution for homeless individuals.

In case studies around the US, many big cities have set up communities of tiny houses. These 'micro home' communities are composed of a village of tiny homes lined up in rows. Others follow a scattered site approach, where the houses are integrated into the community neighborhoods. These homes are generally stand alone or in small groups. But what they all have in common is their financially feasible approach to providing affordable housing for the poor and homeless.

### ZONING

Organizations looking to build a tiny home village must first consider where such homes can be legally located or risk ending up in a situation similar to the group, 'Occupy Madison,' in Madison, Wisconsin. In their case, the tiny houses are allowed to sit on church property in groups of three, they may also park on the side of the road, but problematically, these homes have to be moved every 48 hours.

In Seattle, a village requires anywhere from 6,000 to 30,000 square feet on a vacant lot, which translates generally to 15 to 34 houses. The range changes depending on the number of tiny homes and the commonly shared facilities to be distributed there. Such shared facilities often include a kitchen, meeting space, counselors' offices, storage space, donation and security huts, plumbing, shower, toilets, and laundry facilities.[129]

## COST

Occupy Madison's building costs for tiny homes ran up to $5,000 each. But even in the most expensive campaigns—such as one in Austin, Texas, where they are planning to build a 6-million-dollar tiny home park—that price does not come close to the cost taxpayers' monies are used per year towards homelessness. For example, in Austin, Texas, residents pay over $10 million a year toward homelessness.[130]

Another option that communities have chosen to fund these villages is through crowd-funding and private donations.

## LOW INCOME HOUSING INSTITUTE (LIHI)

LIHI specializes in developing, opening, and operating affordable housing for low-income, homeless, or formerly homeless individuals in Washington State. One of the

---

129 Lee, Sharon. "Tiny House Villages in Seattle: An Efficient Response to Our Homelessness Crisis." Shelterforce, June 4, 2019.

130 Lundahl, Erika. "Tiny Houses for the Homeless: An Affordable Solution Catches On." Charter for Compassion, n.d.

branches they operate in oversees several tiny home villages. They have nine villages in and around Seattle, Washington and two more in Olympia, Washington.

LIHI Tiny Home Village[131]

"Each tiny house has electricity, overhead light and a heater. Each tiny house village has kitchen and restroom facilities, onsite showers and laundry, a counseling office, and a welcome/security hut where donations of food, clothing, and hygiene items can be dropped off."[132]

131  Photograph. Low Income Housing Institute, n.d. https://lihi.org/tiny-houses/tiny-house-village/.
132  "Tiny Houses." Low Income Housing Institute, June 19, 2019.

## DIGNITY VILLAGE

Dignity Village began in the early 2000s as both a camping protest and by a collective of homeless activists looking for a viable alternative to sleeping in the rough. The collective of homeless individuals then campaigned to be registered as a nonprofit as they moved from location to location. Dignity Village now boasts that it is the longest-existing, continually operating, city-sanctioned Homeless Village in the United States.[133]

In September of 2001, Dignity Village moved to their final location in Sunderland Yard, near Seattle, Washington, a city owned leaf-composting facility. The beginning set-up was like a campsite, with tents and tarps laid out everywhere. Slowly, through volunteers and residents, a collective of permanent, four-walled, tiny houses were built. Funds for the village was provided through donations of either building materials or cash. The village is composed of forty-three basic-dwelling structures that can host 50–60 residents.

The city contract for Dignity Village stipulates a two-year limit for residents. This can be extended for residents in positions of leadership.

---

133 "Dignity Village." Dignity Village, n.d.

The residences each come with a bed and propane heater. There are generally no utility hook-ups, those units that do have electricity must be approved by a member vote, and typically for medical reasons. The houses do not have running water. There are two shared sinks, several portable toilets, and one shower for the whole village.

## UPKEEP

The villagers pay $35 per month toward facilities to cover operating expenses. This payment is typically thought of as their 'insurance payment.' Operating costs include electricity, water, Internet, waste removal, and port-a-potty services. Besides the fee collected from residents, the village supplements its operating costs with entrepreneurial efforts. They have raised money through plant sales, tie-dye tee-shirt sales, and flea markets. For several years, through a partnership, they ran a hot dog stand, dubbed Dignity Dogs.

Unlike other typical villages, Dignity Village is pet-friendly and will allow their residents to bring in and live with their pets. They also allow homeless couples to live together.

The Five Basic Rules of Dignity Village are:[134]

---

134 Ibid.

- No violence toward yourself or others.
- No illegal substances or alcohol or paraphernalia on the premises or within a one-block radius.
- No stealing.
- Everyone contributes to the upkeep and welfare of the village and works to become a productive member of the community.
- No disruptive behavior of any kind that disturbs the general peace and welfare of the village.

## SCATTERED VERSUS NON-SCATTERED

Although the non-scattered site approach has been highly successful for both Dignity Village and LIHI, it can be a difficult approach for people to commit to. People in the homeless community may refuse housing that they feel ostracizes them and puts them in a category separate from the larger community where they live.

Those who have tried the scattered site approach have generally asked homeowners to put a tiny home in their backyard. To attract homeowners to such a proposition, the city bears the cost of building the tiny home and makes the homeowners the landlords. In Boston, the "plug-in" home is on the more expensive side as it costs about $50,000 to build and includes a stove, toilet, queen bed, and desk. The tiny home is then ready to be rented out to low-income individuals.[135]

Another tiny home community in the vein of the scattered-site approach is, A Tiny Home for Good.

## A TINY HOME FOR GOOD

A Tiny Home for Good, Inc. is located in Syracuse, New York, where they build and manage affordable, safe, and dignified houses for the homeless. The nonprofit's founder, Andrew Lunetta, was inspired to start the organization at a young age. He was living in Austin, Texas and working at homeless shelters when he noticed a disturbing trend. People moving out of the shelter ended up returning a month and sometimes just a week later. He noted that the city of Austin's affordable housing availability and options were, like many other places, dire. The cheapest rent, for the poorest of the poor, was often $300 to $400 a month, and rarely was this housing code compliant, or the roommate situation was not ideal.

"I started asking these individuals who were staying at the shelter what they were looking for. And really, I thought that they were just kind of describing a tiny home: a place that

---

135  Howard, Miles. "You Can't Just Put Homeless People in Tiny Houses."
     The Outline, May 22, 2018.

had their own bedroom, their own bathroom, no roommate situation, and kind of place close to services," said Lunetta.

His idea for a tiny house nonprofit launched from there. In 2015, he got the ball rolling with a small organization that campaigned for start-up funds. By the next year they started building.

### PROPERTY ACQUISITIONS

A Tiny Home for Good's process of finding space to build included scouring potential properties across Syracuse. They seek vacant city lots with lots of zoning codes appropriate for building single-occupancy tiny homes.

Unlike other areas whose main struggle with building tiny homes was finding property to build on, vacant land is the one thing Syracuse doesn't lack.

"When we started, I was really under the impression that we would have access to this land, where the city and the county would be excited to give us this land so that we could put these houses on and get them back on the tax roll."

Lunetta and his team was asked to inform the neighbors in the projected neighborhoods of the city where they thought the tiny homes would be a good fit. That was when the project ran into trouble. They experienced major pushback from communities who worried about how the residents of these tiny homes would impact their communities. Subsequent town hall meetings produced enough calls to elected officials that the city reversed its decision and said they could no longer donate the land. The lack of neighborhood approval became the first barrier, even before any talk of permits.

"I think this idea that a young organization with no track record wanted to come and start offering housing to homeless individuals was really scary for neighborhoods," said Lunetta.

This did not stop the team who had faith they could turn around the negative perceptions of the community in another way. Once they realized they weren't going to get land donated, they made the decision to go out and purchase a piece of land instead. They found a private landlord who owned vacant land close to downtown Syracuse and purchased it for $2,800 to begin.

## THE BUILDING

Tiny Homes for Good are built in partnerships with volunteers and local contractors. Each home is 300 square feet. They are equipped with all the amenities of a modern home including: beds, bedding, bedside tables, lamps, laundry supplies, toiletries, microwave, coffee pot, kitchen utensils, towels, stove, kitchen table, and chairs.

"It's not transitional living or a little cubby space, it's a home. The goal is that people can stay there for a little while, or they can stay there for the rest of their lives, and all the stuff that they'll need is right there," said Lunetta.

Previously, the initial layout in the tiny homes was like a studio apartment with one large room with a kitchen, bedroom and dining space, then a room blocked off as the bathroom. After feedback from residents, the new layout will feature a ten-foot tall enclosure and the room will be partitioned so the bedroom is separate. In addition, to save energy, the units will be completely air-sealed and use a mechanical air-exchanger.

"Our first units were 260 square feet. Each unit costs about $28,000. Whereas now we've bumped it up to 306 square feet, and It's about $32,000. That's because we've added washers and dryers in each unit and separated the rooms. Residents said that they'd like a washer and dryer on site, and they didn't want to open the door and be right in their living room. So, we created a small foyer space," said Lunetta.

## RESIDENT TREATMENTS AND HOUSING FIRST

Residents are referred to A Tiny Home for Good from local case management organizations, or the VA hospital. Potential residents fill out a short application. The only action that bars housing is if someone has an arson conviction. Other than that, anyone can put in an eligible application if they are homeless and have some form of income. Once the application is filed, they are put on the waitlist.

The lease agreement is one year and based upon reported income. If the resident is on a fixed income, the rent is 30 percent of their monthly income. If the person is employed, rent is $300. Utility costs are covered for the first year, then if a resident decides to renew their lease, they take on the utility charges.

Each resident is connected to outside care organizations in the Syracuse area who manage professional care. Similar to a Housing First model, there are no special requirements in the lease that require that a resident must complete a certain number of case management hours each week, nor are there rules prohibiting them from alcohol.

In addition to a Housing First model, Tiny Home for Good buildings follow a scattered site approach with tiny homes built at a maximum of six per site. Some sites have only two or three.

"I feel like a village or a big place with 20 to 25 Tiny Homes deals with more of a stigma. So, you're pointing to this community of 25 Tiny Homes saying that's where the homeless people live. Whereas we have places where there are three tiny houses, and there's three people who are living in these tiny homes. They're a part of a neighborhood and it's not as if it's something different. They're simply renters in the neighborhood," said Lunetta.

## GOING FORWARD

By February 2020, A Tiny Home for Good plans on opening their 21st home. Since their struggle to find land in 2015, the process has been much smoother based on two factors: reputation and private land.

Based on the impact they've had in the community the past couple years, it is much easier for the nonprofit to point to what the tiny homes actually look like and that the residents are not the scary drug addicts, criminals, and crooks but just a neighborhood resident like anyone else.

"It's gotten much, much better simply because I can point to houses that have been built. I can bring our current residents to some of these neighborhood meetings. They have the opportunity to explain their story and share about what's going to happen. I think that's really important. I'm glad that we're in a position where I can point to success. It's made everything so much easier," said Lunetta.

While A Tiny Home for Good has been extremely successful in terms of the lives impacted and changing the stereotype of homelessness in these neighborhoods, that doesn't mean Lunetta wouldn't have done anything differently the first time around.

"I really think that having your ducks in a row, owning the property, and having the money [in place] before advertising building tiny homes for individual stakeholders, is the way to go. So, making sure you have everything in order, with renderings and so on before you publicize that you're doing the build," said Lunetta.

### CHANGING THE DEMOGRAPHIC

Lunetta believes that with a few changes, his model could be applicable to a youth and young adult centered tiny home experience.

"[Right now,] Tiny Homes doesn't have a requirement for case management. That might be really helpful for youth and young adults, as the needs are probably greater. I think that the case management is much more effective given the trauma is more immediate than someone who's been homeless 10–20 years who might just need case management to maintain," said Lunetta.

He also believes that while his Tiny Homes offer an experience that can be a permanent living space for their residents, in the case of younger residents, the tiny homes would better serve a transitional living experience.

"Tiny Homes are well suited for [transitional living] just because they're easy to move into in a day or in two days. They can be freshly painted, and new floors installed, if needed, and easy to turn around for transition," said Lunetta.

### TAKEAWAY FOR YOUNG ADULT HOMELESS

Non-scattered tiny home villages may not be so problematic and a sticking point for the young adult homeless. Given their age these younger individuals may better handle the close acquaintances with those that are in a similar age range and conditions. In this sense, the tiny homes village option would serve as a transitional step to permanent housing.

Scattered tiny homes models including, A Tiny Home for Good, are seen as affordable, leave a small ecological footprint, and can be constructed with the help of volunteers. The Tiny Home for Good model could be tweaked to accommodate youth and young adults through higher support structures, with a case management system that was readily available to address the needs of the young renters. Other changes beneficial to youth would be to change the model so it is transitional rather than permanent and enables youth and young adults on the path of upward mobility through opportunities to pursue education and jobs while they are securely housed.

# ADVOCACY AND OUTREACH

---

## ROLE OF THE GOVERNMENT IN CHRONIC HOMELESSNESS

The government is ideally supposed to serve as a social safety net for those who fall through the cracks. They have the power, through the people's will, to set legislation that can either protect or criminalize the life of homeless people, as well as set the budget for programs that can serve as solutions to finding housing, support, and meeting needs. Because of their power, it is critical to have a government that is well-informed and aware of all the solutions out there, as well as what is most effective, and what information out there may, in fact, be erroneous, a myth, or even have detrimental effects.

"When you look at the Western countries, Canada, Europe, Australia, New Zealand, the US has the highest number of per capita homeless. We have this high number because those other countries have social housing, universal health care, and a reasonable education system. These social initiatives are not unrelated: homelessness is just the symptom," said Dr. Sam Tsemberis, "It's like a wound that's bleeding and homelessness is the blood that's oozing out of the wound, and we see it, it's the most dramatic part. It's not enough just to sponge up the blood. We really have to heal the wound, if we want to stop the bleeding."

In this case, taking care of the wound means solving the structural problems that contribute to homelessness. This would involve some very powerful value-driven decisions in this country. But that change is completely possible. When we look around the globe at many other countries, we are among the worst of an enlightened Western society when it comes to dealing with this chronic issue.

What is needed is the most effective housing models, money backing these programs, and ultimately the policy driven by government to make those changes.

"The government is us, right? The political will is the will of the people. We have to decide that we want different social structures as a matter of values," said Tsemberis.

## CRIMINALIZATION OF HOMELESSNESS

The government has the power to do a lot of good for minorities that face higher barriers and setbacks. Unfortunately, stereotypes, myths, and misinformation can lead to legislation that can hurt the progress of the homeless. One of the most detrimental moves the government can make is legislation that makes the homeless existence a burden. There are necessary activities that homeless groups undertake to survive on the streets, yet the governmentally imposed associated fines and burdens can make it even harder for these groups to achieve housing. The governmental mentality further perpetuates a negative perception towards homeless individuals as well. These acts can come out in many forms but generally, these criminalization measures fall under these four categories:[136]

- Carrying out sweeps (confiscating personal property including tents, bedding, papers, clothing, medications, etc.) in city areas where homeless people live.
- Making panhandling illegal.
- Making it illegal for groups to share food with homeless persons in public spaces.
- Enforcing a "quality of life" ordinance relating to public activity and hygiene.

---

136 "Criminalization." National Coalition for the Homeless.

The outcome of such measures is increased barriers to providing services for the homeless. In addition to the daily survival the homeless pursue in their attempt to find security and sustenance, the addition of a criminal record could make the already difficult process of finding housing, a job, or eligibility for services nearly impossible.

According to the National Coalition for the Homeless, homeless individuals aren't the only ones negatively affected by this: "Additionally, the criminalization of homelessness adds to an already overburdened criminal justice system by detaining individuals who have not committed serious crimes. One night in jail costs 3 times more on average than a shelter, and law enforcement is both unprepared and incapable of handling homelessness and related issues."[137]

Yet, there are inherent protections in the constitution that would seem to run counter to this criminalization.

- The 1st amendment, protection of freedom of speech, should protect speeches that involve begging or panhandling.
- The 4th Amendment, protection from unreasonable search and seizure, suggests Law Enforcement directed

---

137 Ibid.

to destroy a homeless person's belongings is unconstitutional.

- The 8th Amendment, protection from cruel and unusual punishment, implies imposing criminal penalties for engaging in necessary life sustaining activities could fall under the category of a cruel and unusual punishment.
- The 14th Amendment, protecting citizenship, due process, and equal protection, means vague statutes that do not give a person notice of prohibited conduct and encourage arbitrary enforcement are unconstitutional.

## THE HOMELESS BILL OF RIGHTS

The homeless face violence and increasing criminalization in areas across the nation. Groups such as the National Coalition for the Homeless believe that based on years of research and advocacy that added protections are needed to preserve the civil rights of this demographic. Their idea is to draft a Homeless Bill of Rights that clearly lays out protections and rights of these individuals.

According to the National Coalition for the Homeless, a homeless bill of rights would grant privacy and property protections, allow the opportunity to vote and feel safe in their community without fear or harassment, provide broad access to shelter, social services, legal counsel, quality education for the children of homeless families, protection against segregation, and revisit laws targeting homeless people for their lack of housing rather than their behavior, as well as restrictions on the use of public space.

Many cities, states, and territories have begun to take up this call and pass homeless rights legislation. Many, such as Traverse City, Baltimore; Madison, Wisconsin; and Connecticut have passed bills of rights through their legislature in an effort to protect the vulnerable. In Connecticut they passed a document back in 2013 detailing seven rights:[138]

- Move freely in public spaces, including on public sidewalks, in public parks, on public transportation and in public buildings without harassment or intimidation from law enforcement officers in the same manner as other persons.
- Have equal opportunities for employment.
- Receive emergency medical care.
- Register to vote and to vote.
- Have personal information protected.
- Have a reasonable expectation of privacy in his or her personal property.
- Receive equal treatment by state and municipal agencies.

---

138 Keyes, Scott. "Connecticut Passes Landmark 'Homeless Person's Bill Of Rights' Law." ThinkProgress.

Their bill has served as inspiration for communities, cities, and states across the nation hoping to add similar protections to their laws.

## ADVOCACY AND AWARENESS

### CAMPAIGNING

Many teams have launched campaign efforts hoping to provide rights and tackle key issues that affect the homeless demographic. Helping to extend campaigns from the national level into communities is one of the most effective ways to raise awareness and turn action into progress. For example, one of the initiatives the National Coalition for the Homeless has undertaken is called, 'Homeless People Deserve Food Too.' The campaign tackles the criminalization of food sharing. The criminalization of food sharing programs was established in over twenty cities back in 2013, in an effort to prohibit individuals and groups from sharing food with people experiencing homelessness.[139]

The argument against food-sharing programs is that they are detrimental to the system because there is no opportunity to connect homeless individuals with services they may require.

---

139 "Share No More: The Criminalization of Efforts to Feed People in Need." *Share No More: The Criminalization of Efforts to Feed People in Need*. National Coalition for the Homeless , October 2014.

Yet, that sets up the expectation that meals are provided only after homeless individuals sign up for services or management. Often these individuals may not have positive feelings or experiences with shelters and food pantries. Therefore, it is important to meet them where they are when it comes to such a basic necessity.

Homeless people already face a wide variety of complex and overlapping issues without a system set up that exploits and denies basic needs.

Young adults and youth who live on the streets face a subset of more specific problems as well as the larger campaign efforts to help the homeless. One such group that campaigns for these issues is Covenant House. They have campaigns for foster care reform, anti-trafficking of minors, employment and education programs, and transitional housing programs.

## Y2Y EFFORTS

Many of the groups that specialize in one-on-one interaction with homelessness, such as shelter and housing programs, are the frontrunners in the fight for legislation toward their interest groups. Y2Y Harvard Square has initiatives addressing city and statewide efforts. Their team assembles research and gives testimony regarding specific bills up in the community that could impact youth homelessness. The ability to have youth and young adults who have or have had personal experience with homelessness can be extremely powerful in the State House, on both a logical and an emotional level. They can share their stories and give advice on what efforts would best help them directly.

"We have a variety of different things going on throughout the course of the year. Most recently, we went with guests and staff to the Statehouse to talk to legislators about specific bills that are impacting our young people. Our residents are really involved at citywide and statewide efforts around homelessness, partly because they're just already extremely engaged, and are kind of making connections through the program," said founder of Y2Y, Sarah Rosenkrantz.

Together, Y2Y's guests and student volunteers collaborate on advocacy initiatives to raise support for, and awareness of, young adult homelessness. Using program data, they will approach lawmakers and inform public understanding to promote policy decisions that direct increased attention and resources toward this pressing issue. At the same time, their advocacy programming gives young adults experiencing homelessness the opportunity to become leaders in creating social change and to bring their own stories to light.

## GRANTS AND PROGRAM FUNDING

The United States Department of Housing and Urban Development (HUD) awards grants and monetary assistance each year to communities administering homeless assistance and housing programs at the local level. Both public projects run by government offices and private nonprofits are eligible to apply.

Community organizations have the opportunity to apply for grants such as the Emergency Solutions Grant (ESG) formula grant program that funds street outreach, homelessness prevention and diversion, emergency shelter, and rapid re-housing. Another competitive grant, the Continuum of Care (CoC) program, funds permanent supportive housing, rapid re-housing, transitional housing, coordinated entry, and demonstrations.[140]

The Youth Homelessness Demonstration Program (YHDP) is one example of this. The program is a new initiative by HUD that as of August 29, 2019, has awarded $75 million in grant funding to 23 selected communities in hopes of ending youth homelessness. The communities chosen will develop coordinated community plans to prevent and end youth

---

140 "FY 2020 Appropriations: HUD's Homeless Assistance Grants and Affordable Housing." National Alliance to End Homelessness, 2019.

homelessness and award funding to projects that align with their plans.[141]

Other HUD assistance includes four program accounts in appropriations bills that go towards housing the most insecure individuals. They provide housing assistance in the form of voucher programs and rent subsidies:[142]

- Tenant-Based Rental Assistance (TBRA)—this includes the Housing Choice Voucher (HCV) program ("Section 8"), Housing and Urban Development-Veterans Affairs Supportive Housing (HUD-VASH) vouchers, and Family Unification Program (FUP) vouchers.
- Project-Based Rental Assistance (PBRA)—formerly known as "Project-Based Section 8," this program provides rent subsidies for many privately – owned affordable housing programs.
- Public Housing accounts:
- Operating Funds—used by Public Housing Authorities for day-to-day costs.
- Capital Grants—used for larger scale building repairs or maintenance.

---

141 "FY 2018 (Round 3) Youth Homelessness Demonstration Program Community Selection Announcement." HUD Exchange. US Department of Housing and Urban Development, August 29, 2019.

142 "FY 2020 Appropriations." National Alliance to End Homelessness, 2019.

There are many benefits to entering the grant process. When awarded, besides the monetary benefit, government grants can provide credibility to nonprofits and attract other donors. The government can also provide support in the form of partnerships along with the grant or connections to other resources. Depending on the efforts and results, the government could come to regard the nonprofit as an expert in the field and give them a voice on policy changes.

The extreme difficulty to this avenue of support is that grant applications are a lengthy and arduous process. They often require 80–200 work hours to complete for nonprofits and hiring a professional grant writer can cost a couple thousand dollars. By the time government grant competitions are announced, there may only be 4–8 weeks to turn in an application. In addition, if awarded, the grant can lead to increased oversight by the government who wants to see if their funds are achieving the intended result. An award may also lead to reduction in other revenue sources who see the funds awarded by HUD and believe the nonprofit does not need more.

There are factors that the government looks for and can increase a business's chance of being awarded a grant. Eligible and competitive communities that are likely to be awarded grants demonstrate such factors as a successful history of grant-seeking. In the past, the non-profit may have been the recipient of a corporate, family, or community foundation award. Another factor includes demonstrating the capacity and qualifications necessary to implement the grant in a way that aligns with the government plans. Along with this, the reputation of the organization, a history of successful projects and outcomes, as well as doing the research to show an evidence-backed project all help with competitiveness of the applicant.[143]

### TAKEAWAYS

Government resources, policies, and legislation have the power to critically impact the state of the youth and young adult homeless community. But often, it takes the voice of the people through advocacy, campaigning, and activism to rally around, lobby government officials and put issues such as homelessness farther up their priority list.

Grants and funding can add meaningful assistance to programs and nonprofits who also rely on the goodwill of the community to keep running.

---

143 Stombaugh, Heather, and JustWrite Solutions. "Is Your Nonprofit Ready to Apply for a Government Grant?" The Balance Small Business. Dotdash Publishing, April 13, 2019.

Some of the most impactful voices of influence come from the young adults who have personally experienced homelessness. Programs such as Y2Y's advocacy projects put these individuals in a place where their voices are heard and have a direct affect on the future of homelessness.

# ONE PERSON CAN MAKE THE DIFFERENCE

---

*"We think sometimes that poverty is only being hungry, naked and homeless. The poverty of being unwanted, unloved and uncared for is the greatest poverty. We must start in our own homes to remedy this kind of poverty."*

–MOTHER TERESA

As mentioned in ,'The Root of the Problem' chapter, Kate* and her three sons had a soft spot for troubled kids in need. Initially, her sons brought home a couple friends from school who needed a place to stay, and it caught on that her home was an open place to stay. Over the course of six years, she had over thirty-two boys stay at her home. Boys stayed there varying from a few days to a couple of weeks, and even three years. Kate was not a foster parent, youth homeless shelter, or transitional living home. But the impact she had on these kids' lives was exactly what they needed.

"Part of the reason [my housing accommodations] was never on paper is because it just would have taken too long for me to get certified and jump through whatever hoops and these kids needed a place tonight. And I didn't want to become their foster parent on paper. My goal was always to get them in a more stable place. I didn't want the money." Kate said.

She would make a phone call to the boy's guardians, parents, or whomever they reported to notifying them the boys were at her home, even if it was for one night.

"Every single one was contacted. And I told all of these people, 'Sounds like you've had a rough night with your son. He knows my door's open. This is my address. This is my phone number. If you don't want him to stay here, I will send him home now. If you're okay with him staying here. You're welcome to come over. See where I live. Please come by. You guys can talk on the front porch, in the backyard, whatever if you just want to visit or you want to talk on neutral turf.'"

In her experience, no parent ever came over to see where their kid was staying.

The boy who stayed with Kate the longest was Brandon*. He stayed at her house for three years. He had a tough home life with a dad who had remarried and was out of the picture, and a mom who needed psychiatric care and lived with her parents. He was half-Caucasian and half African American and he believed because of this neither grandparents wanted anything to do with him.

"I did contact both of his parents, and both sets of grandparents. And none of them ever wanted anything to do with him. He truly believed that if he was not staying with me, he would be on the street and my house was his only recourse to homelessness."

"And no matter who was in the house, every week, I would go to each kid and I would say what is one thing I can do for you this week? And every week, he would look at me, and he would say, 'Mama, you let me sleep in your house. If I was not here, I would be on a park bench,'" said Kate.

"We said that every single week," Kate adds. "Brandon, what's something I can do for you this week.' And he would say if you have to do one thing, 'I would love homemade bread,' or something that he knew I was going to do anyway."

## HOUSE RULES

Although this was not their permanent home or housing situation, that doesn't mean Kate's house was a free-for-all. Kate's rules were few but hard and fast: there would be no girls at the house if she wasn't home. It was not a co-ed living situation. She only had boys. The other rule was that they had to go to school. That worked for many of these kids. She was listed as their contact and emergency contact information at school. There were times though that she ran into trouble with accountability with some of the boys. One time one of the counselors at the high school called her and told her a kid put her down as his emergency contact. The school hadn't seen him all week. This was on a Friday at noon and at this point, he was living part time with Kate and part time with his mom. Kate responded to the counselor and said he'll be there in an hour.

"I call him and someone he'd been [hooking up] with answered the phone. She said, 'he's sleeping,' and I responded, 'I don't care. This is mama Kate; can you tell him I need to talk to him right now.' She responded, 'Well, can't you wait?' And I said, 'No, this can't wait, you wake him up. So, she woke him up. And I basically raised six kinds of pain with him and said, 'You want to come to my house this evening and stay for this weekend?' He said, 'Of course.'"

Kate followed this up with the directive that if he didn't go to school immediately, he would not be coming over this weekend. So, after some grumbling the boy went. He showed up at the guidance counselor's office and had them call Kate, so she knew he made it.

"It's crazy that [coming to my house] was like the biggest leverage I had to begin with."

The boys as a group held each other accountable. Her rules were pretty short, but very specific. One rule was no matter what time the boys came in, and no matter what time they left they had to go hug Kate and tell her they were at her house. This way she knew who was at the house, and would know whether they were drunk, high, or sick. Kate recounted there were times the boys showed up sick but wouldn't tell anybody. It wasn't because they were on drugs or alcohol, they just didn't want to be a burden to anyone. The rules summed up were that they would not drink alcohol, use weed, no girls in the house, and they would go to school.

"Basically, that's all they needed. If they could do those things and go to school, actually, like they were probably going to be okay," Kate said.

While not everyone has the means or ability or huge heart it takes to support at-risk or homeless young adults, and youth in the way Kate has, it doesn't mean we are powerless to help. Some forms of help include more time and are more energy intensive such as fostering a kid and continuing to support them after they age out of foster care. Other ways are more short-term, things such as educating yourself and others, monetary donations, volunteering time, reaching out to people in positions of power who can impact this often-unseen need of homeless youth. All these actions can make an impact.

### FOSTER CARE PARENT

Many young adults and youth end up homeless after traumatic at home experiences or aging out of foster care. One of the most powerful ways people can make a difference for this homeless population is through offering them the care and support they need but are not receiving in their lives. This path is not simple emotionally, socially, and in terms of time, but this challenging volunteer opportunity is one of the most rewarding paths one can take.

Qualifications to become a foster parent listed on The National Foster Parent Association site include but are not limited to:[144]

---

144 "Becoming a Foster Parent." The National Foster Parent Association – Becoming a Foster Parent, n.d.

- Meet the physical, emotional and developmental needs of a child.
- Provide 24-hour care and supervision on a daily basis.
- Be able to care for yourself financially without the child's stipend.
- Be flexible, patient and understanding.
- Have a sense of humor.
- Have a home free of fire and safety hazards.
- Complete a criminal/protective services background check.
- Have the ability to work as a member of a team.

Both single and dual-parent families make great foster parents. Most states and regions also welcome same-sex partners as foster parents. The foster care agencies help vet you to decide if you meet the qualifications and can provide care that satisfies the physical, emotional, and developmental needs of the child.

Every day there are kids who don't have the opportunity to live in safe and providing homes. When you become a foster care parent you open your heart and home to a child who is in crisis.

## VOLUNTEER

Many local organizations offer opportunities to volunteer. Depending on where you go, you could spend your time helping social services, teaching life skills, packing boxes to distribute food across the community, or serving hot food in a food kitchen. Other people use their specific skills to help in non-conventional ways, such as giving a haircut, or helping homeless people transition into working a job, or paying the bills.

## LEGISLATION

Another way to make an impact involves getting involved with government. At the state level, you can write letters to your Senator urging them to put funding toward specific programs in the DHHS department or about supporting certain types of youth homeless housing models.

At the local level, many decisions that affect funding for youth homeless programs are made. By reaching out to your representatives you can raise advocacy for this group and put them as a priority for future bills being passed regarding their funding or status. You can attend town council meetings regarding these issues and programs for the homeless.

## CAMPAIGNING

You can call your local homeless shelters and find out what items they may need. Then with this information in hand, contact local scout troops or civic organizations to organize fundraising events, such as food drives, to provide these items.

Other people have written letters to the editor of their local newspapers about their community and the homeless problems they face.

## SHOW RESPECT

One of the simplest ways to change the mindset on homelessness is by how individuals respond when they see it. Instead of treating these people like they are invisible or subhuman, nod and say, 'Good morning.' For many people, the internal loss of dignity they feel can be harder than the external loss of physical objects.

When you pass homeless people asking for money, one of the best approaches can be to give them food, water, and your time instead. You can carry gift cards to grocery stores or fast food chains. Others give small things, such as gloves and hats in the winter or a clean shirt to hand out in the sweltering heat of the summer can go a long way. Little things such as socks, granola bars, water bottles and other items are always useful to carry and benefit the homeless.

Create jobs. If you are in a position to give a homeless person a job, do it. Whether this means a consistent job such as a cashier or clerk, or paying them to do a household task such as mow the lawn.

## DONATIONS

Youth and young adult homelessness is one of the worthiest causes to support. Shelters are in constant need of donations—not only financial, but clothes, bedding, and toiletries. Some suggested items include:[145]

- Winter weather clothing (such as hats, mittens, coats, and boots).
- New underwear and socks.
- Travel-sized hygiene items (toothpaste, soap, etc.).
- Professional clothing (a hurdle to overcoming homelessness is looking presentable at job interviews).
- First aid items (such as Neosporin, Band-Aids, antibacterial cream, and hand sanitizer).

---

145 wikiHow. "How to Help the Homeless." wikiHow. wikiHow, May 16, 2019. https://m.wikihow.com/Help-the-Homeless#_note-4.

- Secondary medical items (such as sunscreen, heavy duty lotions like Bag Balm, allergy medication, and tissues).
- Bus passes (great for helping them get to job interviews).
- Linens (i.e. twin sheets, towels, pillows and pillowcases).

If you have the financial means, any of the organizations listed below are worth looking into:

A Tiny Home for Good
www.atinyhomeforgood.org

Covenant House
www.covenanthouse.org

Eva's Initiatives
www.evas.ca

Low Income Housing Institute (LIHI)
Website: www.lihi.org

National Alliance to End Homelessness
endhomelessness.org

Pathways to Housing
www.pathwayshousingfirst.org

Treatment Foster Care Oregon (TFCO)
www.tfcoregon.com

Rapid Results Institution
www.rapidresults.org

YES Omaha
www.yesomaha.org

Y2Y Harvard Square
www.y2ynetwork.org

This is not necessarily an exhaustive list. One needs to research in his or her area to see if there are places to help. Plus, new organizations may be created.


**THE HEART OF THE MATTER**

Kate's house was almost always full.

"One of my guy friends had come over one time, and there were like nine boys there. He brought a laptop. And he said, while he looked at this collection of interesting kids, 'Can I leave my laptop here.' He was concerned about it. And I said, 'Watch this.' I put $127 and 12 cents on the middle of the dining room table, and I put a deck of cards on it. I said, 'This is how much I've put here.'

"The only reason I remember is because I counted it out very specifically it was all small random bills and change. I said, 'I will leave this here for two months and they may move it. But two months from today, mark my words, there will be $127 dollars and 12 cents. These bills exactly. No matter how desperate these kids, no matter how broke these kids get. They may ask me for money, but these dollars will be here.'

"And 10 weeks later, he came back. Someone said, 'Mom, I moved the stack of money,' just as he was walking in.' I hadn't said anything to the kids about it.

"No one stayed at my house because we had luxury accommodations. One bedroom was mine. Nobody, I mean nobody, camped in my bedroom. So that left me with three bedrooms, two couches, and three recliners. And usually all of them were full. But I believe that it was less about crashing on the couch. Yes, it was about having a place to stay so they were not on a bench, but it was more than that."

Kate's experience showed her that, for these kids, finding a home is not just about a place to sleep. She believes the reason the kids kept coming back to her place specifically was because her family gave them more than that.

"I think they just wanted somebody who would hold them accountable. And who would love them and go to bat for them, but who would also hold their feet to the fire and say, you need to be the best version of you that you can be today."

# EPILOGUE

———

The issue of youth homelessness, like adult homelessness, is complex and multi-layered. That does not mean it is insurmountable. As we have seen in the pages of this book, there are many innovators who seek to challenge the status quo, from a single woman who opened her home to homeless youth, to a man who saw a need for housing and looked for ways to meet that need.

The game-changers in starting a social movement at the grassroots level are the ones who saw this problem and didn't let adversity stop them from addressing homelessness in a sustainable way. The innovators interviewed in this book created housing models, emergency youth shelters, and collective community movements to house the homeless.Many of the programs laid out in this book are already adapted to youth and young adults. They all hold certain elements in common that make them well suited for the younger displaced person's needs. These programs emphasize security for youth and young adults so that they feel safe. They acknowledge that emergency housing for the young is not ideally permanent. Although stability in a housing program can be beneficial, this is not the same as the need for permanent housing. Making sure there are pathways to economic mobility through support to attain education and income are essential to supply youth and young adults with the opportunities they deserve.

Youth and young adults are at a critical point in their lives when it comes to addressing trauma and roadblocks in the way of their own personal growth and health. They benefit from the extra care that case managers, therapists, and advisors can give them as they learn to navigate the adult world.

The progressive programs that are created for homelessness, such as Housing First models and Tiny homes have the potential to be adapted and shaped into youth-centric solutions. This can be accomplished by applying elements that many of the youth-centric models above have done**additional care and support, community living, and transitional timelines are just some of the factors to be considered.

## HOW CAN YOU HELP?

Perception of what homelessness is provides the beginning. Who do we see when we see someone without a place to go at night? Hopefully, this book lays out just the tip of the iceberg of reasons youths end up on the streets and how our perceptions can aid or hinder what choices we make so that we help, rather than hinder, where youth end up at night. A kind word and acknowledgement to someone you see going through this situation, and above all, cultivating a sense of empathy, is key to progressing along the path toward understanding one another's situations.

Education. What are the resources available in your area of the country? When we know, we are then empowered to make choices that will aid in moving forward toward a better understanding of solutions and how to help.

Connections. Look to other programs across the country who provide models for how to attack gaps in programming and in presenting solutions that will help communities in financially sustainable ways.

**Advocate.** There are big ways and little ways that you too can impact young adult homelessness. Whether this is donations, starting your own organization, every young person deserves stability, love, and acceptance in the place they call home.

Even if you only come away from reading this book with a better understanding of why youth fall into homelessness and the challenges they face, you have taken a giant step forward. I hope you will continue on the path to challenging yourself to be part of the solution for our young homelessness population.

# APPENDIX

---

**INTRODUCTION**

"Homelessness in America." National Coalition for the Homeless. National Coalition for the Homeless , n.d.

Morton, Matthew, et al. "One in 10 Young Adults Experience Homelessness During One Year." *Chapin Hall*, Chapin Hall.

"The State of Homelessness in America." National Alliance to End Homelessness. Accessed August 23, 2019.

**CHAPTER 1: THE FACE OF HOMELESSNESS**

"28 Dec 1873, Page 5 – The New York Times at Newspapers. com." Newspapers.com. Accessed July 01, 2019.

Barbara Duffield and Phillip Lovell, "The Economic Crisis Hits Home: The Unfolding Increase in Child and Youth

Homelessness," National Association for the Education of Homeless Children and Youth and First Focus, December 2008.

Bell, Alison, and Douglas Rice. "Congress Prioritizes Housing Programs in 2018 Funding Bill, Rejects Trump Administration Proposals." Center on Budget and Policy Priorities. July 20, 2018. Accessed July 09, 2019. https://www.cbpp.org/research/housing/congress-prioritizes-housing-programs-in-2018-funding-bill-rejects-trump.

Blasi, Gary, Dan Flaming, Michael Dear, Paul Koegel, Paul Tepper, Daniel Warshawsky, and Jennifer Wolch. "What Led to the Rise of Homelessness." KCET. April 06, 2017. Accessed July 01, 2019. https://www.kcet.org/shows/socal-connected/the-rise-of-homelessness-in-the-1980s.

Capps, Kriston. "Nationwide, Homelessness Plunged Under Obama." CityLab. November 18, 2016. Accessed July 09, 2019. https://www.citylab.com/equity/2016/11/homelessness-obama-trump/508223/.

Henry, Meghan, Anna Mahathey, Tyler Morrill, Anna Robinson, Azim Shivji, Rian Watt, and Abt Associates. *The 2018 Annual Homeless Assessment Report (AHAR) to Congress*. Report. The U.S. Department of Housing and Urban Development. 2018.

Horowitz, Evan. "Poverty Drives Homeless Rates? Not so Fast – The Boston Globe." BostonGlobe.com. August 24, 2016. Accessed July 01, 2019. https://www.bostonglobe.

com/2016/08/24/poverty-drives-homeless-rates-fast/1fv-vSKgNUg4l5TfqbdEGrM/story.html.

Jackson A. A Place Called Home: A History of Low–Cost Housing in Manhattan. Cambridge, MA: MIT Press; 1976.

Jones, Marian Moser. "Creating a Science of Homelessness During the Reagan Era." *The Milbank Quarterly* 93, no. 1 (March 2015): 139–78. https://doi.org/10.1111/1468–0009.12108.

Katz, Michael B. *The Undeserving Poor: From the War on Poverty to the War on Welfare.* New York: Pantheon Book, 1989.

National Academies of Sciences. "The History of Homelessness in the United States." Permanent Supportive Housing: Evaluating the Evidence for Improving Health Outcomes Among People Experiencing Chronic Homelessness. July 11, 2018. Accessed July 01, 2019.

Newspapers, Tony Pugh – McClatchy. "Obama Vows to End Homelessness in 10 Years."

McClatchy DC. June 22, 2010. Accessed July 09, 2019. https://www.mcclatchydc.com/news/nation-world/national/economy/article24585973.html.

Ramírez, Kelsey. "Proposed 2020 HUD Budget Sees Meager Increase from Last Year's Proposal." HousingWire.com. March 11, 2019. Accessed July 09, 2019. https://www.housingwire.com/articles/48396-proposed-2020-hud-budget-sees-meager-increase-from-last-years-proposal.

Sand, Barbara. "Number of Homeless Families Climbing Due To Recession." Center on Budget and Policy Priorities. October 11, 2017. Accessed July 01, 2019. https://www.cbpp.org/research/number-of-homeless-families-climbing-due-to-recession.

"The Boxcar Boys and Girls." Hobo Life in the Great Depression. 2016.

"The State of Homelessness in America." National Alliance to End Homelessness. Accessed July 09, 2019. https://endhomelessness.org/homelessness-in-america/homelessness-statistics/state-of-homelessness-report-legacy/.

Vertz, Laura L. *Publius* 15, no. 1 (1985): 183–85. http://www.jstor.org/stable/3329956.

Wiltz, Teresa. "A Hidden Population: Youth Homelessness Is on the Rise." The Pew Charitable Trusts. July 7, 2017. Accessed July 09, 2019. https://www.pewtrusts.org/en/research-and-analysis/blogs/stateline/2017/07/07/a-hidden-population-youth-homelessness-is-on-the-rise.

## CHAPTER 2: THE ROOT OF THE PROBLEM

Abramo, Allegra. "Youth Often Become Homeless Just after Leaving Juvenile Detention. Can Washington State Really Stop It?" The Seattle Times. April 25, 2019. Accessed July 09, 2019. https://www.seattletimes.com/seattle-news/homeless/youth-often-become-homeless-just-after-leaving-juvenile-detention-can-state-really-stop-it/.

Administration on Children, Youth and Families, Family and
Youth Services Bureau: Street Outreach Program Data
Collection Project Final Report (April 2016).

"Camp Rules." Transcript. In *Queer Eye*. Netflix. February
7, 2018.

Gleeson, Jill. "A Home Full of Hope: Bobby Berk." EDGE
Media Network. November 27, 2014. Accessed July 09,
2019. https://www.edgemedianetwork.com/style/
home//168738.

"Homeless Youth Aged out of Foster Care." Interview by Mark
Horvath. YouTube. September 2, 2013. Accessed July 9,
2019. https://www.youtube.com/watch?v=TbquG1H0CXQ.

"Homeless Youth: NCH Fact Sheet #13." National Coalition
for the Homeless, August 2007. https://www.national-
homeless.org/publications/facts/youth.pdf.

"Homeless Youth Was in over 25 Foster Care Placements
before He Ran Away." Interview by Mark Horvath. Youtube. September 11, 2013. Accessed July 9, 2019. https://
www.youtube.com/watch?v=NsA5dvpJYyg.

"James Was Living with Him Mom until Drugs Forced Him
out into the Chicago Streets." Interview by Mark Horvath.
YouTube. September 19, 2013. https://www.youtube.com/
watch?v=9mzGuBWR03Q&list=PL51CPD51hq2Qk3M5T-
V50Gac9GsyHouSa3&index=24.

"Oakland Homeless Family." Interview. YouTube. August 10,
2017. Accessed July 9, 2019. https://www.youtube.com/
watch?v=zo5kHGeWULM.

Pilnik, Lisa, Darla Bardine, Laura Furr, Meghan Maury, Melissa Sickmund, Naomi Smoot, and Jason Szanyi. *Addressing the Intersections of Juvenile Justice Involvement and Youth Homelessness: Principles for Change.*Report. March 2017.

U.S. Department of Health and Human Services(a). Youth with Runaway, Throwaway, and Homeless Experiences… Prevalence Drug Use, and Other At-Risk Behaviors, 1995. Volume I (the Final Report, including the executive summary) is available for $48.15; the Executive Summary alone is available for $3.15. Order from the National Clearinghouse on Families & Youth, P. O. Box 13505, Silver Spring, MD 20911–3505; 301–608–8098.

"What's Your Origin Story? with Bobby Berk." Interview. *Getting Curious with Jonathan Van Ness* (audio blog), July 24, 2018.

"Youth Homelessness Overview." National Conference of State Legislatures. June 18, 2019. http://www.ncsl.org/research/human-services/homeless-and-runaway-youth.aspx.

## CHAPTER 3: CHOOSING THE STREETS

Glier, Ray. "The Problem of Youth Homelessness Is Not the Fault of the Youth, Experts Say." Youth Today. February 22, 2019. https://youthtoday.org/2019/02/the-problem-of-youth-homelessness-is-not-the-fault-of-the-youth-experts-say/.

"Our Issue." True Colors United.

Shay, Kylyssa. "Why Don't Homeless People Use Shelters?" Soapboxie. January 27, 2017. https://soapboxie.com/ social-issues/why_homeless_people_avoid_shelters.

"Why Some Homeless Choose the Streets Over Shelters." Interview. *Talk of the Nation* (audio blog), December 6, 2012. https://www.npr.org/2012/12/06/166666265/why-some-homeless-choose-the-streets-over-shelters.

**CHAPTER 4: THE DEGREE DIFFERENCE**

Bauer-Wolf, Jeremy. "Homeless College Students Struggle to Find Lodging, Food over Winter Break." Inside Higher Ed. January 15, 2019. Accessed July 10, 2019. https://www.insidehighered.com/news/2019/01/15/homeless-college-students-struggle-find-lodging-food-over-winter-break.

Duffield, Barbara, Patricia Julianelle, and Michael Santos. *The Most Frequently Asked Questions on the Education Rights of Children and Youth in Homeless Situations.* Report. September 2016. http://nlchp.org/wp-content/uploads/2018/10/McKinney-Vento_FAQs.pdf.

"Education of Homeless Children and Youth." National Coalition for the Homeless, September 2009. https://www.nationalhomeless.org/factsheets/education.html#footnotes).

Edwards, Earl J. "Advice from a Formerly Homeless Youth." Education Week. February 20, 2019. Accessed July 09, 2019. https://www.edweek.org/ew/articles/2017/04/18/i-was-a-homeless-student-and-invisible.html.

Goldrick-Rab, Sara, Jed Richardson, Joel Schneider, Anthony Hernandez, and Clare Cady. *Still Hungry and Homeless in College.* Report. April 2018. https://hope4college.com/wp-content/uploads/2018/09/Wisconsin-HOPE-Lab-Still-Hungry-and-Homeless.pdf.

*Higher Education: Actions Needed to Improve Access to Federal Financial Assistance for Homeless and Foster Youth.* Report. United States Government Accountability Office. May 2016. https://www.gao.gov/assets/680/677325.pdf.

"Homeless College Student Shares Her Story and Some Hip Hop on Its 44th Anniversary." Interview by Mark Horvath. YouTube. August 11, 2017. https://www.youtube.com/watch?v=JoY25s5L0VQ.

"Homelessness on Campus." Interview by Lee Cowan. CBS News. January 20, 2019. Accessed July 9, 2019. https://www.cbsnews.com/news/homelessness-on-campus-the-toughest-test-faced-by-tens-of-thousands-of-college-students-in-america/.

"Homelessness: Targeted Federal Programs." *Homelessness: Targeted Federal Programs.* Federation of American Scientists, October 18, 2018. https://fas.org/sgp/crs/misc/RL30442.pdf.

"McKinney-Vento Act: Two-page Summary." SchoolHouse Connection. August 1, 2018. Accessed July 10, 2019. https://www.schoolhouseconnection.org/mckinney-vento-act-two-page-summary/.

Miller, Madison. "Average Cost of College in America: 2019 Report." ValuePenguin. April 23, 2019. Accessed July 10, 2019. https://www.valuepenguin.com/student-loans/average-cost-of-college.

Morton, M.H., A. Dworsky, and G.M. Samuels. *Missed Opportunities: Youth Homelessness in America.* Report. Chapin Hall, University of Chicago. November 2011. http://voicesofyouthcount.org/wp-content/uploads/2017/11/Chapin-Hall_VoYC_NationalReport_Final.pdf.

"What's Your Origin Story? with Bobby Berk." Interview. *Getting Curious with Jonathan Van Ness* (audio blog), July 24, 2018.

"Young Homeless Girl Is a College Student 'flying a Sign' in Pasadena." Interview by Mark Horvath. YouTube. August 20, 2012. https://www.youtube.com/watch?v=Vb-khD-srDQ8.

## CHAPTER 5: IN THE ROUGH

"Although Graphic, Arien Shares the Realities of What Women Have to Endure While Living on the Streets." Invisible People. June 17, 2016. Accessed July 08, 2019. https://invisiblepeople.tv/videos/arien-young-homeless-woman-hollywood/.

"Behavioral Health among Youth Experiencing Homelessness." *InFocus*3 (October 2015). October 2015. Accessed July 9, 2019.

Dank, Meredith, Jennifer Yahner, Kuniko Madden, Isela Bañuelos, Lilly Yu, Andrea Ritchie, Mitchyll Mora, and Brendan Conner. "Surviving the Streets of New York Experiences of LGBTQ Youth, YMSM, and YWSW Engaged in Survival Sex." *Surviving the Streets of New York Experiences of LGBTQ Youth, YMSM, and YWSW Engaged in Survival Sex*. Urban Institute, February 2015. https://www.urban.org/sites/default/files/publication/42186/2000119-Surviving-the-Streets-of-New-York.pdf.

"Domestic Violence and Homelessness." *Domestic Violence and Homelessness*. ACLU, n.d.

Edmondson Bauer, Elizabeth, Kris Bein, and Cat Fribley. *College-Aged but On the Streets: Young Adults Who Experience Homelessness and Sexual Violence*. National Sexual Assault Coalition. Resource Sharing Project. May 2017. http://www.resourcesharingproject.org/sites/resourcesharingproject.org/files/YoungAdultsWhoExperienceHomelessnessandSexualViolenceMay2017.pdf.

Greene, Jody M., Susan T. Ennett, and Christopher L. Ringwalt. *Prevalence and Correlates of Survival Sex Among Runaway and Homeless Youth*. Issue brief. September 1999. https://www.ncbi.nlm.nih.gov/pmc/articles/PMC1508758/pdf/amjph00009-0102.pdf.

"Homeless Youth & Sexual Violence." National Sexual Violence Resource Center Jones, Carolyn. "Abuse, Violence Common among LGBT Homeless Youth, Study Finds."

EdSource. April 25, 2018. Accessed July 08, 2019. https://edsource.org/2018/abuse-violence-common-among-lgbt-homeless-youth-study-finds/596734.

Kipke, Michele D., Thomas R. Simon, Susanne B. Montgomery, Jennifer B. Unger, and Ellen F. Iversen. "Homeless Youth and Their Exposure to and Involvement in Violence While Living on the Streets." *Journal of Adolescent Health*20, no. 5 (1997): 360–67. doi:10.1016/s1054–139x(97)00037–2.

Lippy, Carrie, Sydney PK, Emily Hsieh, Shannon Perez-Darby, and Connie Burk. "King County Youth of Color Needs Assessment." *King County Youth of Color Needs Assessment.* The NorthWest Network, May 2017. https://static1.squarespace.com/static/566c7f0c2399a3bdab-b57553/t/597fd3ed893fc098807bb872/1501549553222/Youth of Color Needs Assessment_ Final Report.pdf.

Marks, Kathy. "Australian Teenagers Filmed Themselves Setting Fire to Homeless Man." NZ Herald. NZ Herald, September 18, 2017. https://www.nzherald.co.nz/world/news/article.cfm?c_id=2&objectid=3579533.

"Mental Illness." National Institute of Mental Health. February 2019. Accessed July 10, 2019. https://www.nimh.nih.gov/health/statistics/mental-illness.shtml.

"Pregnant Homeless Girl Talks about "survival Sex" for Homeless Youth." Interview by Mark Horvath. YouTube. September 27, 2010. https://www.youtube.com/watch?v=gFlgirdLiu4.

Tarr, Peter. "Homelessness and Mental Illness: A Challenge to Our Society." Brain & Behavior Research Foundation. January 24, 2019. Accessed July 10, 2019. https://www.bbrfoundation.org/blog/homelessness-and-mental-illness-challenge-our-society.

"Toronto Youth Documents His Life of Homelessness and Addiction | Red Button." Interview. YouTube. August 2, 2017. Accessed July 9, 2019. https://www.youtube.com/watch?v=g4P8PJf4-NY.

"Substance Use Among Youth Experiencing Homelessness." *Substance Use Among Youth Experiencing Homelessness.* 2nd ed. Vol. 20. Nashville, TN: National Health Care for the Homeless Council, 2016.

"Voices of Youth Count: Understanding and Ending Youth Homelessness." Chapin Hall. Accessed July 08, 2019. https://www.chapinhall.org/project/voices-of-youth-count/.

"Vulnerable to Hate: A Survey of Bias-Motivated Violence Against People Experiencing Homelessness in 2016–2017." National Coalition for the Homeless , December 2018. https://nationalhomeless.org/wp-content/uploads/2019/01/hate-crimes-2016–17-final_for-web2.pdf.

Wenzel, S. L., Leake, B. D., & Gelberg, L. (2000). Health of homeless women with recent experience of rape. *Journal of general internal medicine*, 15(4), 265–268.doi:10.1111/j.1525–1497.2000.04269.x

## CHAPTER 6: YOUTH CENTERED SHELTERS

"About Covenant House." About Covenant House. Accessed July 11, 2019. https://www.covenanthouse.org/homeless-charity.

"Crisis Care for Homeless Youth." Covenant House. Covenant House, n.d.

Daniel, Ari. Photograph. *NPR*. NPR, January 6, 2016. https://www.npr.org/2016/01/06/461416400/temporary-housing-for-young-people-by-young-people#mainContent.

"The Homeless Shelter for Young People, By Young People." Interview. Philips Brooks House Association. February 1, 2019. Accessed July 11, 2019. http://pbha.org/stories/watch-pbhas-y2y-harvard-square-the-homeless-shelter-for-young-people-by-young-people/.

## CHAPTER 7: TRANSITION HOUSING MODELS

"Chelsea Foyer." Good Shepherd Services. Accessed July 10, 2019.

"Chelsea Foyer Outcome Study." Chelsea Foyer Outcome Study – CIDI. Accessed July 10, 2019.

"FOR Youth: Quality Assurance." Transforming opportunities for young people. Foyer Federation.

"Foyers." Foyers | The Homeless Hub. Canadian Observatory on Homelessness.

"Promising Strategies to End Youth Homelessness." *Promising Strategies to End Youth Homelessness*. Administration for Children and Families, n.d.

Vimeo. Accessed July 10, 2019. https://vimeo.com/145937823.

## CHAPTER 8: THE HOUSING FIRST MODEL

"California Code, Welfare and Institutions Code – WIC §
8255." Findlaw. Accessed July 10, 2019.

Gulcur, L., Stefancic, A., Shinn, M., Tsemberis, S., & Fishcer,
S. Housing,

Hospitalization, and Cost Outcomes for Homeless Individuals with Psychiatric Disabilities Participating in Continuum of Care and Housing First programs. 2003.

*Housing First Checklist: Assessing Projects and Systems for
a Housing First Orientation.* Report. United States Interagency Council on Homelessness. September 2016.

*Housing First in Permanent Supportive Housing.* Issue brief.
HUD Exchange.

McCoy, Terrence. "Meet the Outsider Who Accidentally
Solved Chronic Homelessness." The Washington Post.
May 06, 2015. Accessed July 10, 2019.

McEvers, Kelly. "Utah Reduced Chronic Homelessness
By 91 Percent; Here's How." NPR. December 10, 2015.
Accessed July 10, 2019.

Montgomery, A.E., Hill, L., Kane, V., & Culhane, D. Housing
Chronically Homeless Veterans: Evaluating the Efficacy
of a Housing First Approach to HUD-VASH. 2013.

National Psychologist Staff. "'Housing First' Reducing Homelessness." The National Psychologist. March 04, 2018.
Accessed July 10, 2019.

Tsemberis, Sam. "Interview to Sam Tsemberis, Creator of the Housing First Program in a Community of USA." Interview. YouTube. Accessed January 20, 2017.

Tsemberis, S. & Eisenberg, R. Pathways to Housing: Supported Housing for Street-Dwelling Homeless Individuals with Psychiatric Disabilities. 2000.

Tsemberis, Sam, Leyla Gulcur, and Maria Nakae. "Housing First, Consumer Choice, and Harm Reduction for Homeless Individuals with a Dual Diagnosis." American Journal of Public Health. April 2004. Accessed July 10, 2019.

**CHAPTER 9: FAMILY INTERVENTION MODELS**

Center for Law and Social Policy. 2003. Leave No Youth Behind: Opportunities to Reach Disconnected Youth, p. 57. *Ending Youth Homelessness Before It Begins: Prevention and Early Intervention Services for Older Adolescents.* Report. July 23, 2009. Accessed July 11, 2019. https://b3cdn.net/naeh/5a3c6b2bf975ee8989_1bm6bhh9y.pdf.

*Family Reconnect: A Path for Youth to Return from Homelessness?* Report.

"Multidimensional Treatment Foster Care." Washington State Institute for Public Policy. December 2018. Accessed July 11, 2019.

National Institute of Mental Health. "TFCO Model vs Group Home Care Outcomes," n.d.

Pergamit, Michael, Julia Gelatt, Charmaine Runes, and Brandon Stratford. *Implementing Family Interventions*

*for Youth Experiencing or at Risk of Homelessness.* Urban
Institute. Urban Institute. November 2016. Accessed
July 11, 2019. https://www.urban.org/sites/default/files/
implementing-family-interventions-for-youth-experi-
encing-or-at-risk-of-homelessness.pdf.

"The American Family Today." Pew Research Center's Social
& Demographic Trends Project. December 17, 2015.
Accessed July 11, 2019.

"Treatment Foster Care Oregon." Blueprints for Healthy
Youth Development. Accessed July 11, 2019.

"What We Do." Eva's Initiatives for Homeless Youth. Accessed
July 11, 2019.

## CHAPTER 10: COMMUNITY CHALLENGERS

S. Rep. No. Committee on Appropriations-115–268 (2019).

Nouvelle, Chloe. "Allentown's 100-Day Challenge to Combat Homelessness." PBS39 WLVT. February 06, 2019.
Accessed July 11, 2019.

Ukiah Daily Journal. "100 Day Challenge on Youth Homelessness." The Ukiah Daily Journal. August 23, 2018.
Accessed July 11, 2019.

## CHAPTER 11: TINY HOMES FOR THE HOMELESS

"Dignity Village." Dignity Village, n.d.

Howard, Miles. "You Can't Just Put Homeless People in Tiny
Houses." The Outline, May 22, 2018.

Lee, Sharon. "Tiny House Villages in Seattle: An Efficient Response to Our Homelessness Crisis." Shelterforce, June 4, 2019.

Low Income Housing Institute, n.d. https://lihi.org/tiny-houses/tiny-house-village/.

Lundahl, Erika. "Tiny Houses for the Homeless: An Affordable Solution Catches On." Charter for Compassion, n.d.

"Tiny Houses." Low Income Housing Institute, June 19, 2019.

### CHAPTER 12: ADVOCACY AND OUTREACH

"Criminalization." National Coalition for the Homeless.

"FY 2018 (Round 3) Youth Homelessness Demonstration Program Community Selection Announcement." HUD Exchange. US Department of Housing and Urban Development, August 29, 2019.

"FY 2020 Appropriations: HUD's Homeless Assistance Grants and Affordable Housing." National Alliance to End Homelessness, 2019.

Keyes, Scott. "Connecticut Passes Landmark 'Homeless Person's Bill Of Rights' Law." ThinkProgress.

"Share No More: The Criminalization of Efforts to Feed People in Need." *Share No More: The Criminalization of Efforts to Feed People in Need.* National Coalition for the Homeless , October 2014.

Stombaugh, Heather, and JustWrite Solutions. "Is Your Non-profit Ready to Apply for a Government Grant?" The Balance Small Business. Dotdash Publishing, April 13, 2019.

## CHAPTER 13: ONE PERSON CAN MAKE THE DIFFERENCE

"Becoming a Foster Parent." The National Foster Parent Association – Becoming a Foster Parent, n.d.

WikiHow. "How to Help the Homeless." wikiHow. wikiHow, May 16, 2019. https://m.wikihow.com/Help-the-Homeless#_note-4.